ONTARIO SPORTS TRIVIA

J. Alexander Poulton

© 2011 by OverTime Books
First printed in 2011 10 9 8 7 6 5 4 3 2 1
Printed in Canada

All rights reserved. No part of this work covered by the copyrights hereon may be reproduced or used in any form or by any means—graphic, electronic or mechanical—without the prior written permission of the publisher, except for reviewers, who may quote brief passages. Any request for photocopying, recording, taping or storage on information retrieval systems of any part of this work shall be directed in writing to the publisher.

The Publisher: OverTime Books is an imprint of Éditions de la Montagne Verte

Library and Archives Canada Cataloguing in Publication

Poulton, J. Alexander (Jay Alexander), 1977–
   Ontario sports trivia / J. Alexander Poulton.

Includes bibliographical references.
ISBN 978-1-897277-72-0

   I. Sports—Ontario—Miscellanea. I. Poulton, J. Alexander (Jay Alexander), 1977– II. Title.

GV585.3.O6P68 2011   796.09713   C2011-906330-1

Project Director: J. Alexander Poulton
Editor: Jordan Allan
Cover Image: Baseball glove: © Bobbiholmes/Dreamstime.com; boxing gloves: © Zedcor Wholly Owned; cyclist: © Václav Volráb/Dreamstime.com; figure skater: © 2011 Ryan McVay/Thinkstock/Photodisc; football: © 2006 Jim Jurica/iStockphoto.com; golfer: © Sergey Kashkin/iStockphoto.com; Hockey Hall of Fame: © 2010 Jeff Whyte/Dreamstime.com; Ivor Wynne Stadium: © 2010 mark.watmough | Creative Commons; track sprinter: © Jupiterimages; all other photos: © Photos.com.

We acknowledge the financial support of the Government of Canada through the Canada Book Fund (CBF) for our publishing activities.

Government of Québec—Tax Credit for book publishing—Administered by SODEC

 Canadian Heritage   Patrimoine canadien

PC: 1

Contents

Introduction **6**

Chapter 1:
The Puck Stops Here **11**

Chapter 2:
Are You Ready for Some Football? **75**

Chapter 3:
More Than Just the Blue Jays **94**

Chapter 4:
Ontario, Basketball's Native Land **108**

Chapter 5:
No Longer Fringe Sports **120**

Chapter 6:
Ontario Olympians **133**

Chapter 7:
Golfing Ontarians **186**

Chapter 8:
A Wide Variety of Pastimes **200**

Notes on Sources **214**

Dedication

To Marvin, Joyce and Alexander

Acknowledgments

I'd like to extend special thanks to all those behind the scenes of this book: editors, accountants, the graphics and administrative staff and the many others who don't often get the credit they deserve. Without them, my words would not make sense, the pages would not be in order, the cover would be blank and this book would never get to the reader.

Introduction

The province of Ontario holds a special place in the history of Canadian sports. In all of the 10 provinces and three territories, athletes and teams from Ontario have produced some of the most memorable sporting moments. From the glory days of the Toronto Maple Leafs and the Ottawa Senators, to the gridiron exploits of the Argonauts, to the world stage at the Olympics, Ontario's athletes have amassed an impressive list of accomplishments.

Naturally, hockey is at the top of that list. Hockey has always been at the centre of Canadian culture, and in Ontario the history of the sport runs deep. Other sports such as golf, boxing, soccer, baseball, basketball and football have all played a pivotal role in the lives of Ontario athletes throughout the last two centuries and in the formation of our country as a whole. Where would the National Hockey League be without the contributions of teams from Toronto and Ottawa, not to mention the countless other amateur leagues and teams that have formed the basis of our hockey culture for so long? The Stanley Cup might have never been created had the governor general not taken a liking to the brand of hockey being played in Ottawa in the late 1800s.

Or perhaps look to baseball. Americans love to claim baseball as their sport, just as Canadians like to think of hockey as our own (which it is, by the way), but with a little research, the Americans' claims that baseball was solely their creation is put to the test. Most historians state that Alexander Cartwright founded modern baseball in 1845 in New York City; however, several years earlier, in 1838 in the sleepy town of Beachville, Ontario, someone wrote a letter to a friend describing a game that closely resembles modern baseball.

Then there is Canada's contribution to the sport of basketball. Even though, yet again, many Americans say that one of their own invented the game, every Canadian knows that James Naismith was born in Canada and always acknowledged that he was from Canada. Born in the small Ontario town of Almonte, Naismith might have developed the game in the United States, but he based basketball on a childhood game that he used to play in the fields around his home.

Looking to football, the CFL has often been ridiculed for being a simple minor league when compared with the mighty NFL, but the history of football in Canada is rich and quite surprising to most people. For example, did you know that the Toronto Argonauts, founded in 1873, are the oldest football team in North America? But it's not just historical facts that make Canadian football exciting. In pursuit of the Grey Cup, teams have played through some of the harshest weather conditions Canada could throw at them. Through rain, ice, mud and fog, players have battled it out on the gridiron for the right to be called the Grey Cup champion since the University of Toronto Varsity Blues won it in 1909. In fact, from 1909 to 1930, only teams from Ontario had taken home the Grey Cup until the Montreal AAA Winged Wheelers broke the provincial streak in 1931. Since 2006, it has been left to the Toronto Argos and the Hamilton Tiger-Cats to represent Ontario in the battle for the Grey Cup, but in 2013, Ottawa will once again return to the CFL for their chance at Grey Cup glory.

As you can see, Ontarians have contributed to many different sports, but as I said earlier, it has been hockey that has held the hearts and minds of Canadians for close to two centuries. Although hockey might have originated in Eastern Canada (more specifically in Nova Scotia), Ontario has been at the forefront of the sport and was instrumental in turning it from a backyard pursuit to the non-official religion of most Canadians. Those early teams—such as the Ottawa Hockey Club, the Toronto Wellingtons and the Queen's University of Kingston hockey club—helped to bolster support for the game when it was still in its infancy and ushered the game into the professional era.

It was also in Ontario that the governor general of Canada, Lord Stanley of Preston, fell in love with the game in the early 1890s and decided that a special cup should be created to celebrate and honour the best hockey team in the Dominion of Canada. So in 1893, he commissioned the creation of the Dominion of Canada Challenge Cup (thankfully later renamed the Stanley Cup) and began a cultural legacy that is as Canadian as the Mounties or snowstorms.

From the creation of the Stanley Cup to today, hockey has been a huge part of what makes up the rich sports culture of Ontario. Wayne Gretzky lived and breathed hockey on his backyard rink in Brantford, the Toronto Maple Leafs personified the game for so many and players like Bobby Orr and Darryl Sittler gave kids everywhere someone to look up to. Through all the good and bad, hockey has entrenched itself into the consciousness of the province and will only get stronger.

While hockey, baseball and football from Ontario have all made an impact on the sporting world, we must not forget about the individual athletes who have made their mark on the national and international stage. People such as Jamaican-born but now proud Ontarian Donovan Bailey, who captured the nation's heart by winning the gold medal at the 1996 Olympic Games in the 100-metre sprint. Ottawa's own figure skater Elizabeth Manley wasn't expected to make it onto the podium at the 1988 Winter Olympics in Calgary, but she put in the performance of a lifetime to win the silver medal. Going back further in time, there is the grand dame of Canadian figure skating, Barbara Ann Scott, who during her time was the most fluid, artistic and widely admired athlete in Canada. Her performance at the 1948 Olympics in London united a nation and even spawned a cult following as women and girls from coast to coast wanted to be just like her.

In these pages, you will find the stories, however brief, of some of the most incredible sporting moments and people to come out of the province of Ontario. From hockey to the Olympics, Ontario sports is a phenomenon that continues to grow and spread as younger generations take to the field and rinks of the province, ready to make their mark on the world and show everyone what Canadians are really made of.

Chapter One

The Puck Stops Here

The Ontario Hockey Association

Before the formation of the National Hockey League and even before the creation of the Stanley Cup, there was the Ontario Hockey Association (OHA). In the winter of 1889, teams from across Ontario met up to play in heated matches that made modern hockey violence look like a schoolyard brawl. The games were less about hockey and more about which city held the bragging rights. Hockey was growing in popularity, and these games were originally meant as simple public exhibitions to familiarize people with the concept and the rules, but when families turned out to see this new sport, they were abhorred to see blood spilled on the ice in the name of a game. At the time, there was no governing body to officiate the playing of the games and to ensure that the rules were being followed. Following the public outcry about the rampant violence, it was finally decided that something had to be done.

In the fall of 1890, representatives from the various clubs met in Toronto and agreed to join together to form an official league called the Ontario Hockey Association. One of the association's founders at that meeting was none other than the Right Honourable Arthur Stanley, also known as Lord Stanley of Preston, governor general of Canada and future creator of the Stanley Cup. He had developed a deep passion for the game of hockey in Ottawa and several of his sons played for the local Ottawa teams.

In the OHA's first year of operation, the league consisted of 13 teams: three teams from Kingston, six teams from Toronto, three teams from Ottawa and one team from Lindsay. Any team could join the league as long as they could pay the $2 registration fee and the $3 annual fee. The first league championship game was played between a team from Ottawa and a team from Toronto, with Ottawa winning the game 5–0.

The Beginnings of Women's Hockey

Lord Stanley was not the only member of his family to contribute to the history of hockey. He passed on that passion for hockey to his eight sons and two daughters. While several of his sons played for the Ottawa Rideau Rebels, the ladies of the house had no place to play the game. So Lord Stanley had the first backyard rink built at his official residence at Rideau Hall. That way, his family could enjoy skating and playing hockey anytime they wanted.

Feeling a little left out, one of Lord Stanley's daughters, Isobel, decided to organize a game of her own in what most historians would agree was the first all-female hockey game. Played on the governor general's backyard rink, photographic evidence exists showing the young women out on the ice. The picture can be found at the National Archives of Canada, and it shows several women dressed in long skirts and holding sticks while chasing the puck. In the photo, Isobel is dressed in white and appears to be trying to get the puck away from an opposing player. Although no date is attached to the photo, it is assumed that it was taken in the winter of 1889 or 1890. Shortly afterward, on February 11, 1891, the first report of a women's hockey game appeared in the *Ottawa Citizen:*

> *A ladies hockey match was played at the Rideau rink yesterday between teams as follows. No.1: Miss MacIntosh, Captain; Miss Wise, Munro, Ritchie, Camby, Jones, and White. No.2: Miss H. Wise, Captain; Miss MacIntosh, Ritchie, McClymont, Burrows, and Mrs Gordon. Number two team won by two goals to none.*

Chivalry to the Rescue

Admittedly, Isobel and her high-society cohorts played hockey as a leisurely pursuit, but these first forays onto the ice gave women across the country the idea that they too could join in the game they loved so much. By the early 1900s, women's games were regular features at community arenas and outdoor rinks, and unlike in other sports such as basketball and golf, women followed the same on-ice rules as men. However, there were still some major differences that were not dictated by rules but by the culture of the time.

Women in the early 1900s were seen as the genteel, fairer sex, and it was expected that they be treated and act as such. Athletics were promoted for women but only sports that did not involve too much strain on their "delicate" frames. Referees at women's hockey games were usually men, and they often coddled the women on the ice as if they were fragile flowers. If a woman—God forbid!—fell, the referee often stopped play and rushed over to offer his hand in assistance. As Wayne Norton details in his book, *Women on Ice*, a referee at a winter carnival in 1906 failed to come to the rescue of a fallen female player and was harshly criticized by the people in the crowd for his ungentlemanly actions.

Unfashionable Miss

This patronizing attitude toward women's hockey was something that women had to deal with well into the 20th century. The clothing they were expected to wear in the early days of women's hockey was laughable by today's standards. Early photos showed little change from their everyday winter clothing of long, heavy, ankle-length skirts, thick sweaters and large tasseled toques—not exactly the key to speed and dexterity in hockey.

Breaking Barriers

It wasn't until World War I that things slowly began to change for women's hockey. Uniforms became a little more practical and gone were the dainty restrictions that women felt they must uphold. The game became faster and more entertaining and, as a result, more women signed up. One of the biggest influences in the sport was without a doubt Fanny "Bobbie" Rosenfeld from Barrie, Ontario, during the 1920s and '30s. Described by journalists at the time as the "superwoman of ladies hockey," Rosenfeld could skate faster than many men and was known for her incredible stickhandling abilities. Her skills on the ice were so far above those of her teammates that she was often left to do most of the work during the game.

Playing for the North Toronto Ladies hockey team, Rosenfeld was the premiere player in women's hockey and brought much-needed attention to the sport. Although she was a passionate hockey player, she also participated in the 1928 Olympics in Amsterdam, winning a gold in the 4x100-metres relay and silver in the 100-metre sprint. But she never gave up on her love of hockey, and in the end, her dedication to all things athletic earned her the unique distinction of being named Canada's Woman Athlete of the half century in 1950 as voted by Canadian sportswriters in print and broadcast journalism.

Despite having pioneers like Rosenfeld, women's hockey was really still a marginal pursuit. It wasn't until 1990 that women's hockey finally achieved a concrete level of respect in the sporting world with the first World Women's Hockey Championships, held in Ottawa. To start the game, a beautiful rendition of the Canadian national anthem was sung by local 16-year-old singing sensation, Alanis Morrisette.

Wearing fluorescent-pink uniforms, the Canadian women took the gold medal and, in doing so in convincing fashion, brought a new respect for their game. Soon after the first world championship and subsequent victories by the Canadian women, names like Hayley Wickenheiser, Cassie Campbell, Danielle Goyette, Jennifer Botterill, Manon Rheaume and Angela James became household names and the inspiration for a whole new generation of women ready to take their sport to the next level.

"Athletic maids to arms! ... We are taking up the sword, and high time it is in defense of our so-called athletic bodies to give the lie to those pen flourishers who depict us not as paragons of feminine physique, beauty and health, but rather as Amazons and ugly ducklings all because we have become sports-minded."

—Fanny Rosenfeld (1903–69)

Who Says Women's Hockey isn't Violent?

The stereotype is nothing new. Men and women alike are guilty of claiming that women's hockey is simply a poor substitute for the more exciting, fast-paced and action-filled men's games. However, the people who make this erroneous claim might not be aware of one game in particular that could change their outlook on women's hockey.

During a game at the 1988 Ontario Women's Provincial Championships of the Ontario Women's Hockey Association (OWHA) between a team from Windsor and a team from Harrow, Windsor forward Trudy Banwell got so upset at referee Angela James that she ended up slamming her to the ice. When linesman Barb Jeffrey tried to step in to help her fallen colleague, she ended up with a separated shoulder as a result of Banwell's fury. After the game, Banwell was arrested and convicted on two counts of assault. For her punishment, she was given two years probation and forced to work 200 hours of community service. On top of it all, the OWHA handed her a lifetime ban.

Puck Split

When rubber pucks were invented in 1872, players did not really appreciate their quirks. Unlike the refined vulcanized pucks of today, the first discs to come out of the factory turned rock solid when on the ice, and when they were slapped with a hard shot or struck a goalpost, they often split into pieces. This happened because the pucks were not made from a single piece of rubber, but a series of laminated layers stuck together.

In one famous incident during the 1902 Stanley Cup finals, Chummy Hill of the Toronto Wellingtons shot the puck into one of the goalposts and the puck split in two, with half flying off into a corner of the rink and the other half ending up in the Winnipeg Victorias net. Amazingly, the referee allowed the puck piece that landed in the net to be called a goal. All was not lost for the Victorias, however, as they went on to win the series and the Cup.

Strange Goal

Fort William–native Jack Adams is immortalized as being one of the greatest coaches in the history of the NHL, and each year the Jack Adams Trophy is given to the NHL's best coach, but few know that Jack Adams got his start on the ice as a player.

During the 1920–21 season, while playing for the Vancouver Millionaires of the Pacific Coast Hockey Association (PCHA), Adams scored one of the strangest goals in hockey history. In a game against their rivals, the Victoria Aristocrats, Adams accidentally scored into his own net. Now, this has happened before in the NHL—the most famous case was that of Edmonton Oilers Steve Smith accidentally scoring on his own net in game seven of the 1986 playoffs, thereby eliminating his team—but what makes Adams' goal so strange is that the referee gave Adams credit for it. It was even marked down as an official goal in the season records, and that one goal enabled him to finish the season at fifth place in scoring.

The One-team Game

On January 2, 1918, three nights before the Montréal Wanderers next scheduled game against the Toronto Arenas, the Wanderers' home stadium, the Westmount Arena, caught fire and burned to the ground. The franchise owners didn't even try to salvage the team's season—the team had already been hit hard by financial problems because of World War I and was having difficulty recruiting solid players. Rather than look for a new rink, owner Sam Lichenstein folded the team, citing $30,000 in losses.

This was just the first season of the NHL, and the board of governors was not prepared to accept the sudden loss of one of its four teams. In only its second month of operation, the NHL was now faced with having a three-team league, a number that did not lend itself well to easy schedules or substantial revenues. The NHL needed to take some sort of action to retain their rights to sue the owners of the Wanderers franchise should any losses occur because of the team's sudden departure. So, rather than simply cancelling the rest of the Wanderers games, the league maintained the normal schedule for another two games while it tried to figure out how to deal with this situation.

On January 5, 1918, the Toronto Arenas took to the ice at Mutual Street Arena for a game against nobody. Six players hopped over the boards and took the opening faceoff, which they won easily. It must have been a surreal sight to see NHL superstar

Cy Denneny casually skate the puck up the ice with minimal effort and push the puck into the open net with one hand. The Arenas left the ice at the referee's whistle and were awarded the single goal and a default win against a team that did not exist.

Lady Byng

If you happened to be a rich noble woman in Ottawa in the early 1900s, sometimes life could get a little boring. Lady Evelyn Byng was the wife of Canada's governor general, Sir Julian Hedworth Georges Byng, and while her husband tended to his duties on Parliament Hill, she would often take in hockey games whenever she could. After attending a number of games, and being a genteel upper-class woman, she appreciated the more refined aspects of hockey, preferring players who showed proper conduct on the ice matched with natural skill. In the hope of promoting these aspects of hockey, she donated the Lady Byng Trophy in 1925 to be awarded to the player who exhibited the best sportsmanship and gentlemanly conduct combined with a high standard of playing ability. The first recipient of the award was Ottawa Senators centre Frank Nighbor.

King Clancy Does it All

On March 31, 1923, King Clancy and the Ottawa Senators travelled to the West Coast to face off against the Edmonton Eskimos of the Western Canada Hockey League in the Stanley Cup finals. In those days, the Cup was not exclusive to the NHL.

Winners from the NHL would play the winners from the Western professional leagues to determine the ultimate Stanley Cup champion.

Clancy was still new to the team at the time and did not get much ice time because most of the starting players were on the ice for almost the entire 60 minutes of the game. Clancy was sitting on the bench for the first game of the two-game, total-point series and only played a few minutes while the Senators went on to win the game 2–1. Again warming the bench for the second game, Clancy did not know that he was about to accomplish one of the most amazing feats in professional hockey history, let alone all of professional sports.

Midway through the first period, Clancy finally got his chance when one Ottawa defenceman went down with an injury. The coach tapped Clancy on the shoulder and he bounded over the boards, eager to take the player's spot on the ice. When the player returned from the dressing room, Clancy was back on the bench. But moments later the other defenceman went down with an injury, and Clancy was again tapped on the shoulder to replace the player while he too went for repairs in the dressing room. When Ottawa's star centreman Frank Nighbor went down, it was Clancy who again stepped in to take his position. If that wasn't enough, when the right winger went to the dressing room for treatment, Clancy happily took his place. Then, in the third period, Clancy was thrown in on the left wing to give the starter a rest. Clancy had managed to play all the positions on the ice except one.

The true test of Clancy's hockey skills came when Ottawa goaltender Clint Benedict was given a minor penalty. At that time in the NHL, all goaltenders were required to serve their own penalties in the box, leaving their nets empty. Benedict skated over to Clancy, casually handed him his goalie stick and said, "Here kid, take care of my net till I get back." For the next two minutes, Clancy tended the Ottawa goal and did not let in a single goal.

Ottawa ended up winning the game and the Stanley Cup. For his part, Clancy went down as the only player in any sport ever to have played every position in a single game, a record that will probably never be broken.

Maple Leaf Gardens

The Toronto franchise that eventually became the Maple Leafs already had two Stanley Cups under their belt by 1926, and the team was the biggest draw in town. The only issue was that the demand far outweighed the supply of tickets to see the team play at the Mutual Street Arena, home to the hockey club since 1917, which could only seat 7500 people. The arena had seen better days, and in 1927, new team owner Conn Smythe decided that another arena had to be built if the team was going to survive and profit. However, a few obstacles stood in his way.

Gathering the requisite finances was difficult for the new owner, but after three years, he was finally ready to break ground on the spot bounded by Carlton, Wood and Church streets. The same architectural firm that designed Toronto's Union Station—Ross and Macdonald—was selected to build the new arena, and on June 1, 1931, construction began on the new Maple Leaf Gardens. Construction was pushed as fast as possible, and on November 12, 1931, just 166 days after ground was first broken, the Gardens was ready to host its first NHL game.

Since its opening, the walls of Maple Leaf Gardens have seen some of the most incredible moments in the history of hockey: the incredible three consecutive Stanley Cups from 1947 to 1949, the glorious 1960s, countless milestones and achievements by some of the best players in the game and, of course, the Leafs final Cup win in 1967.

Maple Leaf Gardens Facts

- Built in 1931, Maple Leaf Gardens took under six months to construct and cost only $1.5 million.

- The arena is located on 60 Carleton Street in downtown Toronto.

- The first game played in Maple Leaf Gardens was between the Toronto Maple Leafs and the Chicago Blackhawks on November 12, 1931. The Blackhawks won the game by a score of 2–1.

- The Blackhawks' Harold "Mush" March scored the first goal in the new building, while Charlie Conacher scored the first Leafs goal.

- The first season the Leafs spent in the Gardens, they ended up winning the Stanley Cup. It was also their first Cup under the Maple Leafs name.

- When Toronto first entered the NHL, they were known as the Blueshirts (1912–18), the Arenas (1918–19), the St. Patricks (1919–27) and then the Maple Leafs.

- In 1948, Maple Leaf Gardens became the first NHL arena to install protective glass around the rink, and soon after, it became mandatory for all arenas in the league.

- The Maple Leafs played their final game in the Gardens on February 13, 1999, suffering another loss to the Chicago Blackhawks, 6–2. They moved into the Air Canada Centre the following season.

Shore Knocks out the Ace

In the 1930s, Boston Bruins defenceman Eddie Shore was always the toughest player on the ice. It was a role that he relished; he would emerge from the Bruins dressing room during home games wearing a black cape, much to the approval of the fans. Shore was not only tough, but he also ranked as one of the best defencemen of his time, being a naturally gifted scorer. However, if not for the quick work of doctors in a Boston hospital, Shore might have been hauled off to jail.

The incident occurred during a game between the Toronto Maple Leafs and the Boston Bruins on December 13, 1933, when things on the ice started getting pretty rough. The Leafs 29-year-old scoring sensation Irving "Ace" Bailey and Shore were both waging battle for the puck when their lives were irrevocably changed in an instant.

Shore was working his way up the ice, flying past the Maple Leafs defender in full stride when he was suddenly tripped by a Leafs player (later identified as Red Horner) and sent sprawling on the ice. Furious, Shore leapt to his feet and attacked Ace Bailey, the first Leafs player in sight. The Leafs star was caught completely off guard by Shore's ferocious check and was sent flying to the ice headfirst. The resounding crack of Bailey's skull hitting the ice could be heard clear across the rink, silencing the normally raucous Bruins fans. Before Shore had time to react, he was blindsided by a Horner-thrown punch that also knocked Shore to the ice. For a brief second, no one moved. There, sprawled on the ice, bleeding from their wounds, were two of the game's greatest talents.

Shore quickly recovered, but Bailey needed much more care. He was immediately taken to hospital, and in those first few hours, Bailey hovered near death. The prognosis was so bad that doctors brought in a priest to administer Bailey's last rites. Furious over Shore's unprovoked assault, Bailey's father jumped on the next train to Boston with a revolver in his hand, ready to kill Shore for hurting his boy. Luckily, Leafs assistant general manager Frank Selke got wind of the plans and tipped off the Boston police about Bailey's father's plans.

Meanwhile, Bailey underwent two difficult brain surgeries that improved his condition but still left the Leafs star teetering on the edge of life. Boston police even went as far as preparing manslaughter charges against Shore should Bailey die in hospital. Fortunately, ever so slowly, Bailey began to recover from his injuries, although he never again played hockey.

At that time, there was no NHL Players Association to ensure that the league's players were taken care of in case they were no longer able to do their job. Players were poorly paid by today's lofty standards, and many athletes worked summer jobs in the off-season just to make ends meet. Suddenly unable to provide for his family, Bailey was left in a difficult position. The NHL decided to step in and help out by organizing a benefit game on February 14, 1934, between the Maple Leafs and a team made up of the rest of the league's best players. The money raised from the game would go toward paying Bailey's medical bills.

Bailey attended the game, and the crowd gave their former star a huge round of applause as he made his way down to the ice to greet the players.

A hush fell over the crowd when Eddie Shore skated over to Bailey to shake his hand. Ever the gentleman, Bailey extended his hand in friendship and the crowd erupted again in applause. Though no longer a player, Bailey remained close to the Leafs organization and worked in the penalty box area, opening and closing the doors, until his death in April 1992.

The Second Longest Game in NHL History

The first longest game in NHL history took place on March 24, 1936, in a playoff game between the Detroit Red Wings and the Montréal Maroons. It lasted into the sixth overtime period, a total of 176 minutes, before Red Wings right winger Mud Bruneteau potted the winning goal.

The second longest game in NHL took place three years earlier in a playoff match between the Toronto Maple Leafs and the Boston Bruins on April 3, 1933, that also lasted into the sixth overtime period for a total of 164 minutes. The game was a defensive sleeper, with neither team scoring a single goal until Leafs forward Ken Doraty put the puck behind Bruins goaltender Tiny Thompson for the game-winning goal.

Very few people know it, but the game between the Bruins and the Maple Leafs was nearly decided by a coin toss. During the break between the fifth and sixth overtime periods, both teams agreed that they should just decide the winner of the game by tossing a coin. To them, the game seemed deadlocked, and if anyone were to score now, it would be because of luck anyway. So, heads, you play for the Stanley Cup, and tails, you lose and head off to the golf course.

But as soon as the fans woke up and realized what the teams were thinking of doing, they began to boo so loudly that the teams abandoned their coin-toss idea for fear that a riot might break out. The fans were tired, but they had not stuck it out to see the winner decided in such an arbitrary manner. With reluctance, the two exhausted teams skated back out onto the ice before Doraty finally put everyone out of their misery.

The One, the Only, King Clancy

During his prime, Francis "King" Clancy was a star defenceman for the Ottawa Senators and the Toronto Maple Leafs. King's playing career lasted from 1921 to 1936, and the nickname suited his over-the-top character perfectly. He was always at the centre of every battle and wasn't afraid to open his regal mouth to make his opinions heard. When his playing career ended, he took over behind the bench for the Toronto Maple Leafs from 1953 to 1956, and Clancy's character only grew in legend and stature.

Conn Smythe, Gambling Man

Okay, so we know that King Clancy played for both the Ottawa Senators and the Toronto Maple

Leafs, but what is even more interesting is how he came to play for the Maple Leafs.

In 1930, Leafs general manager Conn Smythe found himself with a dilemma. The Ottawa Senators, once an elite team of the NHL, were now struggling to pay their bills. Their financial situation had been in decline for several years, and as the 1930 season approached, the team had to take drastic action just to survive. They decided to sell their best player, King Clancy, for $35,000 to the first team to come up with the money. Clancy, the league's best defenceman, had scored 17 goals and 23 assists in 44 games the previous season.

The board members at Toronto Maple Leafs headquarters, however, were not happy with the Senators' asking price and did not want to pony up the money to buy Clancy. Although Symthe pushed the board pretty hard to come up with the cash, the board only offered $25,000. If Smythe wanted to buy Clancy, he would have to invest $10,000 of his own money.

Always up for a sporting challenge, Smythe headed down the racetrack the day after the board meeting and bet $200 on a horse he owned, named "Rare Jewel," which hadn't won a single race all season long. Smythe told himself that if the Leafs were meant to have Clancy, then Rare Jewel would win. On this particular day, Rare Jewel was a 106-to-1 long shot to win, and amazingly, the horse pulled off the stunning upset.

Smythe happily returned to the Leafs' head office the next day and presented the board with the rest of the necessary funds to purchase Clancy's contract. Clancy remained a Maple Leaf until he retired in 1936.

The Kraut Line

Although they played for the Boston Bruins, all three members of the team's infamous "Kraut Line" were originally from Ontario. Woody Dumart, Bobby Bauer and Milt Schmidt had played together in their junior years in the OHA with the Kitchener Greenshirts, where, because of their German ancestry, they were dubbed the Kraut Line. Having played together for several years, the trio had excellent on-ice chemistry. They were noticed by the Boston Bruins scouts, and in 1935, the Bruins signed all three to pro contracts.

By the 1938–39 season, the Kraut Line was fast becoming one of the top scoring lines in the entire NHL and helped lead the Bruins to the Stanley Cup championship. One of their most impressive feats on the ice came during the 1939–40 regular season, when the members of the Kraut Line finished 1-2-3 in NHL scoring. This was the first time in NHL history that all three members of a single line finished at the top of the scoring race.

The Kraut Line did not just play hockey together but were best friends, living together in Boston during the season, and when their country needed them, all three enlisted with the Royal Canadian

Air Force for a tour of duty that lasted from 1942 to 1946. During the war years, because of the climate of unease in the world toward anything German, the Kraut Line changed their name to the "Kitchener Kids," but at the end of the war, the well-known name returned.

First All-Star Game

Although there had been benefit All-Star games before, the first official NHL All-Star game that started the annual tradition was held on October 13, 1947, and was played in Toronto's Maple Leaf Gardens. The Stanley Cup champion Toronto Maple Leafs played against a collection of NHL All-Stars coached by Dick Irvin. The All-Stars won the game by a score of 4–3.

The Sunday Law and Hockey

The Lord's Day Act was a piece of Canadian legislation enacted in 1907 to ensure that Canadians obeyed the Sabbath and refrained from any non-church-related activities. The laws targeted all sports, including the National Hockey League.

On Saturday, March 31, 1951, the Boston Bruins faced off against the Toronto Maple Leafs at Maple Leaf Gardens in game two of the Stanley Cup semifinals. Neither team showed any mercy as the players relentlessly checked, hacked and slashed their way through the game. With each infraction, referee Red Storey was forced to whistle the play dead, separate the players, send the injured off to the dressing room and then wait while arena attendants scraped the pools of frozen blood off the ice. The unending parade to the penalty box and the delays in the game incensed many of the spectators, including William A.H. MacBrien, the Leafs chairman, who descended from his luxury box to yell at the referee for disrupting the flow of the game.

With the score tied 1–1, neither team was ready to give up, and they ignored how banged up and bruised they felt. When the clock ran out on the third period, both teams headed to the dressing room to regain some energy for the overtime period. As most people in the Gardens that night would have predicted, the first overtime period ended with no resolution. At 11:45 PM Eastern Standard Time, both teams returned to their respective rooms and tried to muster up some more motivation to play hockey.

Now into the second overtime period, the game still looked like it was going to go well into the night. As the clock began to tick toward midnight, a group of league officials called the referee over during a stoppage in play. Referee Storey spoke rather animatedly with the officials for several minutes and then told the teams the game was over.

The bewildered teams returned to their dressing rooms, dumbfounded by what had just happened. The officials had told Storey that it was against the law in the province of Ontario to play any organized sports on Sundays, and since the game was inching ever closer to midnight and NHL officials did not want to break the law, they had no choice but to stop the game. The game was declared a no-contest and was continued on Monday night with the score rolled back to zero. The stoppage came out in favour of the Leafs as they finished off the Bruins by a final score of 3–0. Although it was never really enforced, the Lord's Day Act remained a Canadian law until it was finally repealed in 1985.

Before Integration

In the modern, multi-ethnic, multi-national NHL, a player could never be excluded based on the colour of his skin, but for over 50 years in the history of the league, racial discrimination was just another part of the game.

Herb Carnegie, a Torontonian who played for the Québec Aces of the Québec Senior Hockey League during the 1940s, was widely recognized as one of the best players on his team. However, because he was black, he was denied entry into the NHL. Toronto Maple Leafs owner Conn Smythe once told Carnegie, "Herb, I'd sign you in a minute if I could turn you white." The talent was there, but the will from management to break the colour barrier was not. It was not until January 18, 1958, that Willie O'Ree broke through the bigotry when he suited up for the Boston Bruins.

Tough Crowd

On January 22, 1955, the Toronto Maple Leafs played host to the Detroit Red Wings at Maple Leaf Gardens. During the course of the game, a Maple Leafs fan named Irving Tenney thought it would be a good idea to help his team out by inserting himself into the game. At that time, the glass along the length of the boards dividing the fans from the players was not very high, thereby giving unruly fans the opportunity to get within grabbing distance of the players.

Tenney reached out and grabbed the stick of Red Wings' legend Gordie Howe. As the two tussled, Howe's linemate, Ted Lindsay, decided to intervene by slashing Tenney on the shoulder with his stick. Not satisfied that the slash got his point across, Lindsay dropped his gloves, grabbed Tenney and showed him what a real hockey fight was like. Tenney responded by returning a few punches of his own. The referee and linesmen were eventually able to get between the two combatants, and Lindsay was escorted out of the game. Tenney, for his part, was thrown out of the arena, but he had accomplished what he had set out to do—the Toronto Maple Leafs ended up winning the game 4–2.

The next day, Lindsay was sent to the office of league president Clarence Campbell. After a lengthy discussion, Campbell handed Lindsay one of the stiffest penalties ever given in the league, a 10-game suspension. Lindsay immediately protested the decision and launched an appeal with the NHL. The suspension was eventually reduced to four games.

The Greatest Comeback

Although the Philadelphia Flyers and the New York Islanders were able to come back to win a playoff series after being down 3–0, only one team in NHL history has accomplished that same feat in the Stanley Cup final.

In 1942, the Toronto Maple Leafs defeated the league-leading New York Rangers to move into the Stanley Cup final against the Detroit Red Wings. It should have been an easy series for the Buds considering they finished the regular season 15 points ahead of the Wings, who held a losing record of 19–25–4. But for some reason, the Leafs could not solve the Red Wings system and lost three games in a row, putting them just one loss away from losing what they had worked so hard for all season. Spurred on by their coach Hap Day and a seething hatred for all things Detroit, the Maple Leafs battled back in the series with three straight wins of their own and then finished the Red Wings off in the seventh game by a score of 3–1 to win their first Stanley Cup since 1932.

Youngster

Thorold native Armand "Bep" Guidolin loved to play hockey, and as luck would have it, he proved to have some natural talent for the game. Making his way through the ranks, Guidolin eventually joined up with the Oshawa Generals of the OHA and even won a Memorial Cup with the team in 1942. With his hockey career on track at just 16 years old, he figured that maybe if he played hard enough, he'd make it into the NHL in another two or three years if he was lucky. Little did he know that his dreams would come true a lot sooner than he imagined.

Because so many players had left the league to enlist in the army during World War II, NHL teams were in dire need of bodies to fill spaces in the roster. Guidolin was playing well for the Generals, so the Boston Bruins figured that he could survive in the NHL and signed him just before his 17th birthday.

Thus, Guidolin became the youngest player ever in the NHL when he played his first game on November 12, 1942, at 16 years and 11 months old. He played 42 games that season, scoring seven goals and notching 15 assists. In his 10-year NHL career, Guidolin played for the Bruins, the Detroit Red Wings and the Chicago Blackhawks.

What's That in the Cup? OMG!

When the Toronto Maple Leafs won the Stanley Cup in 1964, each player got the trophy for a day and was pretty much allowed to do whatever he wanted with the Cup. Red Kelly decided to take the Cup home and have photographer take a picture of his entire family with it.

Gathering in the living room of the Kelly household on a hot summer day, Kelly thought it would be cute if he placed his naked infant son in the bowl of the Stanley Cup for the picture. The photograph provided Kelly with a wonderful souvenir, but his son also left behind some memories of his own in the Cup.

"He did the whole load in the Cup. He did everything," said Kelly in an interview. "That's why our family always laughs when we see players drinking champagne from the Cup."

Punt the Cup

Long before Red Kelly's son did his business inside the Cup, the "Holy Grail" of hockey had been through a few more harrowing incidents. After the 1905 Ottawa Silver Seven defeated the Dawson City Nuggets in a two-game, total-goals Stanley Cup final by a combined score of 31–5, the players felt they deserved to celebrate their win in style. Celebrating into the wee hours in an Ottawa restaurant, the team had a wee too much to drink and left the establishment in a drunken stupor.

On the walk home, one of the players grabbed hold of the Stanley Cup, took two steps and punted the silver bowl into the nearby Rideau Canal. Not thinking much of it, the players laughed and stumbled merrily on their way, not realizing what one of their own had just done. Fortunately, when the players woke up the next morning, one of them remembered what had happened the night earlier and ran back to the spot where the Stanley Cup had been booted into the river. Luckily, Ottawa can get really cold in the winter, and the players found the Cup sitting on top of the frozen canal, partially covered in snow.

Leave the Cup in Montréal

In the 1947 Stanley Cup finals between the Montréal Canadiens and the Toronto Maple Leafs, Leafs general manager Conn Smythe did something completely unheard of to motivate his team.

The series was living up to its hype as the first-place Canadiens and the second-place Leafs battled hard and traded shutout victories in the first two games. The Canadiens, however, stumbled in the stretch but still managed to win game five in Montréal, bringing the series to 3–2 in favour of the Leafs.

Conn Smythe was fuming after the loss to the Canadiens in game five, berating the players in the dressing room. He then issued an order that the Stanley Cup be left behind in Montréal. Game six was scheduled for April 19 at the Maple Leaf Gardens. The aim of Smythe's order was simple—he felt that his players were simply coasting their way to victory, and by leaving the Cup in Montréal, it would motivate the Leafs all the more not to have to return to Montréal to win it.

The strategy, though counter-intuitive, paid off. Ted Kennedy scored the Stanley Cup–winning goal against the Canadiens late in the third period to give the Leafs a 2–1 victory. Although the Leafs celebrated the victory with the home crowd, their festivities were somewhat muted as the Cup was still sitting in Montréal. In all of the years of the NHL's existence, 1947 is the only year in which a team won the Cup but was not presented with it immediately following their victory.

The Toronto Maple Leaes?

For those people who think the Stanley Cup is a perfect, unblemished holy relic, they need only look a little closer. Sure, the Cup has been dropped, dented, soiled, punted and scratched, but a few mistakes on the Cup are harder to detect. For example, in 1963, the Toronto Maple "Leaes" won the Stanley Cup, though it is not as bad as the 1972 Stanley Cup–winning "Bqstqn" Bruins or the 1981 New York "Illanders."

Honky

Johnny Bower is best known as the legendary goaltender for the Toronto Maple Leafs during their golden era in the 1960s. He was an excellent goaltender who devoted all his time to perfecting his skills, but even the most dedicated professional has to have a little fun. In his spare time, Bower liked to sing, and around the Christmas holidays in 1965, he recorded a song called "Honky the Christmas Goose" to celebrate the season. The first verse was pure poetic genius:

Honky, Honky, the Christmas goose
Got so fat that he was no use,
Till he learned how to blow his nose.
Honk! The way a goose nose blows.

Corny, yes, but the record sold more than 40,000 copies in its first year! A portion of the proceeds went to charity. Bower never released another album.

Murder on Ice

In the entire history of the NHL, only one player has ever died as a direct result of an injury sustained during a regulation game: Minnesota North Star forward Bill Masterton on January 13, 1968.

It may never be proven, but the first possible murder on ice actually happened decades earlier in 1907 in the sleepy town of Cornwall during a game between one of the local teams and their bitter rivals from Ottawa. During the very physical game—as were all the games Cornwall and Ottawa played against each other—the home team's star player, Owen McCourt, was hit over the head with a stick and later died from his injuries. Ottawa's Charlie Masson (yes, the name is strangely close to another infamous murderer) was arrested and charged with manslaughter but was later released when witnesses, because of the fracas that surrounded the play, could not say with certainty that it was Masson's stick that struck the fatal blow.

If he had swung a little harder or had found the wrong spot, former Boston Bruins tough guy Marty McSorley might have also been brought up on charges of manslaughter for his brutal neck-chop on Vancouver Canucks forward Donald Brashear.

The Great Bobby Orr

Wayne Gretzky may own the title of the "Great One," but many people in the hockey world consider Bobby Orr to be the greatest player in the game. His list of accomplishments are long: he remains the only defenceman to have won the league's scoring title (he did it twice), he owns the record for most points (139) and assists in a single season (102) by a defenceman, and every time he stepped on the ice, he was one of the most dynamic skaters to ever play the game—not a bad resumé for a small-town boy from Parry Sound.

Orr got his start in hockey at the age of four, and only a few years later while playing bantam hockey, his talents were already on the radar of several NHL teams. Although other teams were willing to wait until Orr came of age to try to sign him to a contract, the Boston Bruins didn't want another team to have the chance, so they invested in Orr's bantam team to secure his player rights.

To speed up his development, the Bruins fast-tracked Orr through the hockey system and pushed him into the Ontario Hockey Association with the Oshawa Generals at the age of 14; most players in the club are between the ages of 15 and 20.

Orr played with the Generals until he was 18, the legal age to enter the NHL, and he was immediately called up to the Bruins. In 1966, at just 18, he signed his first contract for $25,000, making him the highest paid player in league history at the time.

In his first year in the NHL, he was awarded the Calder Memorial Trophy as the league's top rookie, and he won his first Norris Trophy as the league's best defenceman in 1968 despite being injured and only playing half the season. His prowess on the ice only grew in the following years, and in the 1970 Stanley Cup playoffs, Orr scored the final goal in overtime to win the game, giving the Bruins their first Cup in 29 years.

The boy from Parry Sound was just getting started. In 1971, he set a record that most likely will never be broken—he led the NHL with 139 points and an incredible plus/minus rating of +124. Remember, he was just a defenceman. In 1972, he again scored the Stanley Cup–winning goal, this time against the New York Rangers.

Playing hard every game soon began to take its toll on Orr's body, and by the mid-1970s, he was no longer putting up record numbers and the once-thrilling end-to-end rushes did not have the same flair as they did when he first joined the league. In 1976, he signed as a free agent with the Chicago Blackhawks, but by then, he was no longer the same player. Countless knee injuries had made it painful for him to walk, let alone skate, and as a result, his scoring touch faded. Over the next three seasons with the Blackhawks, Orr managed to play in just 26 games. In 1979, he decided to retire. At the end of his career, Orr expressed no regrets about his aggressive style as a defenceman that cost him his knees and ultimately his career.

"It was the way I played. I liked to carry the puck and if you do that, you're going to get hit. I wish I'd played longer, but I don't regret it. I had a style— when you play, you play all-out. I tried to do things. I didn't want to sit back. I wanted to be involved," Orr later said.

Immediately upon retirement, the normal three-year waiting period for induction into the Hockey Hall of Fame was waived, and in 1979, he became the youngest player to ever receive that honour. Orr also has his own Hall of Fame in Parry Sound and a star on Canada's Walk of Fame in downtown Toronto. Although he was plagued by injuries during his career, his end-to-end rushes and intelligence on the ice are still fondly remembered by those lucky enough to have seen him play, which explains why people never hesitate to call Orr the greatest hockey player ever.

Bobby Orr Highlights

- On March 15, 1969, Bobby Orr recorded his 60th point of the season, surpassing the previous record for a defenceman set by Pierre Pilote of the Chicago Blackhawks in 1964–65.

- On March 15, 1970, Orr scored two goals and had an assist in a 5–5 tie between the Bruins and the Red Wings and became the first defenceman in NHL history to score 100 points.

- On May 10, 1970, Orr scored the overtime Stanley Cup–winning goal on St. Louis Blues goalie Glenn Hall. It was just after he scored the goal that he was sent flying through the air and a photographer managed to snap the iconic photo of Orr with his hands raised, cutting through the air like Superman.

- On November 15, 1973, Orr scored three goals and had four assists to become the first NHL defenceman to score seven points in a single game in a 10–2 victory over the New York Rangers.

- Even more remarkable, on March 12, 1974, Orr became the first player in NHL history to score 100 points or more in five consecutive seasons.

- Bobby Orr won the Stanley Cup twice and also won the Conn Smythe Trophy twice.

Major, Minor

The most exciting play in hockey is the penalty shot. Skater versus goalie, staring each other down across the ice and readying themselves for a five-second battle in which victory goes to the player with the fastest reflexes.

The penalty shot was an invention of the Pacific Coast Hockey Association league president Frank Patrick. Born in Ottawa, Patrick was fed up with deliberate fouls on players with good scoring opportunities, and he introduced the free shot to compensate. The first-ever penalty shot was taken on December 6, 1921, and the first goal scored on a penalty shot was six days later by Tom Dunderdale of the Victoria Aristocrats on goaltender Hugh Lehman of the Vancouver Millionaires. The penalty shot rule was only added to the NHL rulebook before the start of the 1934–35 season. Montréal Canadiens forward Armand Mondou took the NHL's first penalty shot on November 10, 1934, but was stopped by Toronto Maple Leafs goalie George Hainsworth.

Penalty shots today are iconic moments of excitement in a game, but back when they were first introduced, things were done a little differently. Up until the 1940s, two different penalty shots could be awarded: a minor penalty shot and a major one.

A minor penalty shot involved placing the puck approximately 10 metres out from the opposing team's net and allowing a single skater one shot on goal. No driving the net, no dekes, just one hard, powerful shot. The major penalty shot was exactly the same as a regular penalty shot is today: the puck is placed at centre ice and the skater is sent on a classic breakaway.

While the major penalty shot remains, the minor one was eliminated from league play in the 1940s after an incident in which Toronto Maple Leafs left winger Jack Hamilton successfully scored two penalty shots in one game—one of each kind. Boston's Dit Clapper had hauled down Hamilton, and the referee awarded Hamilton a minor penalty shot. The referee, however, suffered what can only be described as a temporary brain malfunction and placed the puck at centre ice. Rather than ask questions, Hamilton snared the puck at centre ice and dashed in on goal, beating the Bruins goaltender with a quick shot. As the Leafs celebrated, the Bruins screamed in protest. Realizing his mistake, the referee placed the puck 10 metres out from the net and allowed Hamilton to take his minor penalty shot. Hamilton blasted it home for another goal. He was only given credit for the second one.

Poor Brad

It's not a record he wanted to have, but despite his best efforts, London native Brad Marsh is in the books as having scored the fewest goals in a career lasting over 1000 games (1978–93). In 1086 games, he managed to light the lamp only 23 times. That's an average of one goal every 47.2 games. Every goal must have been a most cherished event.

You're Fired! No, You're Hired!

Harold Ballard was a special man. He was unlike any other owner in the history of the National Hockey League, and his antics are the stuff of legend. He once printed the jersey names of his players in letters so small that no one could read them, and he was known to hire and fire staff members on a whim. So when Ballard fired Leafs head coach Roger Neilson in March 1979 just a few weeks before the end of the season, no one in the media was really shocked. In the days following the unceremonious firing, the Toronto sports media was abuzz in speculation over Neilson's potential replacement. Ballard always loved a good headline, so he chose to keep the coach's name a secret until the next game when the new coach would walk out of the dressing room.

No one, however, could have predicted what Ballard did next. Two days after firing Neilson, Ballard had one of his trademark changes of heart and decided to re-hire the man he just fired. Ballard, though, still wanted to go through with his big unveiling, so he asked Neilson to wear a paper bag over his head until the opening faceoff. Neilson had way too much class for such cheesy showmanship and refused to give in to Ballard's demands, emerging from the dressing room that night to a standing ovation from fans.

The reconciliation lasted only until the end of the season. Ballard did not give Neilson an extension on his contract, and the two parted ways.

Sittler's Night

No, it wasn't Wayne Gretzky, Mario Lemieux or Sidney Crosby who accumulated an incredible

10 points in one regular-season game; it was Toronto Maple Leafs centreman Darryl Sittler. On the night of February 7, 1976, the Toronto Maple Leafs welcomed the Boston Bruins to town for what was just another regular-season game, but when the night was over, the game went down as one of the most incredible ones in hockey history.

From the outset of the game, it was clear that the Maple Leafs, led by captain Darryl Sittler, were in control of the play. The Bruins had trouble getting the puck out of their own end, let alone getting a play started, while the Leafs' tight forechecking and offence peppered the Bruins rookie netminder Dave Reece with shot after shot, not all of which he managed to save. By the end of the night, Darryl Sittler had racked up 10 points on the frazzled Bruins goalie. The total of six goals and four assists broke the previous record for most points in a single game held by Maurice Richard with eight points. Sittler later recalled that incredible night in an interview.

"As much as the fans fault Reece for what happened, it was simply a night where every shot and pass I made seemed to pay off in a goal. I hit the corners a couple of time, banking shots on off the post. He really didn't flub one goal," Sittler said.

For his efforts in goal that night, Reece was saddled with the unfortunate nickname Dave "In the Wrong Place at the Wrong Time" Reece.

The Great One

From an early age, the Gretzky family knew that young Wayne had a special talent when it came to hockey. He put on his first pair of skates at the age of two and quickly learned the subtleties of the game on the backyard rink that his father Walter built for him at his Brantford suburban home (dubbed "Wally Coliseum").

Every day, young Wayne could be found outside practicing no matter what the weather, and it paid off. Before even entering his teens, Gretzky was already breaking records and gaining the attention of the hockey world. In one season at the age of 10, Gretzky scored an amazing 378 goals and added another 139 assists in 82 games with the Brantford Nadrofsky Steelers. At only 4-foot-3, Wayne couldn't play the physical game that many other, larger kids were being taught to play by their coaches. Fortunately, Wayne looked at hockey in a different way than other players. His father taught him that the player who could see several moves ahead of the opponent always had the advantage, even if he was much smaller. Gretzky practiced drill after drill on his backyard rink, skating, shooting and visualizing how the game was played, trying to perfect his strategy. Sometimes his father braved the cold weather to practice with his son, teaching him the fundamentals of the game.

The practice paid off—the young phenom continued to amass points and break every record. In no time, word of young Gretzky's exploits began to spread, and curious onlookers began to fill up the tiny arenas where he was playing. However, being in the spotlight was not something that Gretzky was used to. During one exhibition game where a large crowd gathered to see him, Gretzky did not put any effort into his game and left the crowd a little disappointed. After the game, Wayne learned another lesson from his father that stayed with him for the rest of his life.

"My father said, 'I don't ever want to see you do that again. All these people came to see you play. You have to be at your top level every night, whether it's an exhibition game or game seven!'" said Wayne, looking back at that as a defining moment in his career. "That always stuck with me. I knew then that I was on display."

Throughout the years, Wayne Gretzky has rarely disappointed both on and off the ice. From the backyard rink to the NHL, he used those lessons to become one of the greatest offensive hockey players and the most prolific record breaker in hockey history.

As did many young stars before him, Gretzky collected his fair share of criticism entering the NHL. A lot of good things were being said about him, but it was the few voices of discontent that ate away at the thin-skinned Gretzky: he was too small, too frail, he wouldn't be able to score goals playing against men twice his size—and so on. In response,

Gretzky just concentrated on his game and quickly silenced all the naysayers.

The Edmonton Oilers were the lucky team to land Gretzky's services, and in his first season, he made his mark by scoring 51 goals and adding 86 assists for a total of 137 points, and he was just getting started. Sure, he wasn't big enough, strong enough or fast enough, but he read the game like no one else before him. Gretzky's additional talent was making his opponents focus entirely on him, opening up the ice for the rest of the team. For other superstars through NHL history, the challenge for their teammates was to get the puck to the Richards and Howes because they could carry the puck to the net themselves. Gretzky played outside those old rules and was 10 times more dangerous for it.

For those lucky enough to have seen him play, it was like watching a rocket scientist on the ice. His passes were a work of art, his shots were aimed like a sniper and he was always in the right place to make a pass or to take the shot. However, the most entertaining position Gretzky took on the ice was behind the net. That area colourfully came to be known as "Gretzky's office," where size and strength didn't matter. Behind the net, with his eyes uncharacteristically pointed down so his opponents couldn't tell were he was looking, Gretzky distinguished his teammates by the colour of their uniforms. His was a new breed of hockey that the fans fell in love with and still talk about to this day.

Gretzky went on to break or set almost every possible record of significance in hockey and continues to hold or share 61 records despite having retired from the game in 1999. Below are just a few of his career highlights of 20 years on the ice.

Gretzky's Long List of Accomplishments (Both Official and Unofficial)

- Gretzky started playing competitive hockey at age six, and by the time he was 13, he had scored a total of 1000 goals.

- When he retired in 1999, Gretzky held and shared 61 individual NHL records. Amazingly, only one of his records has fallen: Gretzky's record of 15 regular-season overtime assists has since been passed by three players: Nicklas Lindstrom (16), Adam Oates (17) and his old Edmonton teammate, Mark Messier (18).

- Wayne Gretzky finished his career with a 1.92 points-per-game average. Only Mario Lemieux, who was retired at the time, had a better points-per-game average. However, when Lemieux came back out of retirement in 2000 and played until the 2005–06 season, his points-per-game average dropped to 1.88 before he retired again midway through the 2005–06 season. The drop in goal production by Lemieux gave the record back to Gretzky, and he didn't even have to do anything.

- Gretzky is the only player to record over 200 points in one season (and he did it four times).
- He holds the record for most career goals with 894 and most career assists with 1963, for a record 2857 points.
- During his career, he amassed 37 three-goal games, nine four-goal games and four five-goal games.
- Gretzky holds the record for the longest point-scoring streak at 51 consecutive games during the 1983–84 season. During the streak, he scored 61 goals and 92 assists. Yes, that's 153 points in 51 games!
- Gretzky has the most 100-or-more point seasons at 15.
- He is the youngest player to score 50 goals in a season (19 years, 2 months).
- He has the most points by an NHL player in his first year: 137. However, because Gretzky had played in the professional World Hockey Association (WHA) before he joined the NHL, he was not considered a rookie that year, so the rookie record belongs to Teemu Selanne with 132 points.
- In a career that lasted 20 seasons, you might imagine Gretzky had amassed quite a few pieces of silverware along the way. On top of three Stanley Cups, he holds the record for the most

MVP awards with nine Hart trophies, the most scoring championships with 10 Art Ross trophies, five Lady Byng trophies for sportsmanlike play, five Lester B. Pearson trophies as the NHLPA's most outstanding player, and two Conn Smythe trophies as the Most Valuable Player in the playoffs.

- Wayne Gretzky lent his name to a trophy that is given out annually to the Western Conference winners of the Ontario Hockey League (OHL). The corresponding trophy of the OHL East is called the Bobby Orr Trophy.

- On top of all his accomplishments, Gretzky was also given an honourary doctorate in law from the University of Alberta in 2000 and has been a member of the Order of Canada since 1984, although he did not receive his medal until 1998 because the Order was always given out in December, right in the middle of the hockey season.

- Wayne Gretzky's final game in Canada came on April 15, 1999, in Ottawa. Fans of the Ottawa Senators switched allegiance for a moment and cheered for several minutes at the end of the game for hockey's greatest player. They chanted "one more year" and gave Gretzky a Canadian send-off he would never forget. The game ended in a 2–2 tie.

- At the 2000 All-Star game in Toronto, it was announced that the NHL was going to retire

Gretzky's famous number 99 league wide. This was the first time in hockey history that any player had received such an honour.

- Gretzky also has the most career playoff goals and assists. Over his 20-year career, Brantford's favourite son appeared in 208 playoff games and tallied an impressive stats sheet: 122 playoff goals and an incredible 260 assists for a total of 382 points. One-time teammate and friend Mark Messier takes second place with 109 goals, 186 assists and 295 points in postseason play.

- Wayne Gretzky made a one-time appearance on the daytime soap opera *The Young and the Restless* in 1982. He played a Mafia goon and had only one line in the entire show: "I'm Wayne from the Edmonton operation."

- Gretzky appeared on television again in 1989 as host of *Saturday Night Live*, producing one of the most cringe-inducing skits ever, called "Waikiki Hockey," where Wayne actually, and unfortunately, sang a Hula hockey song:

    Mona luckahiki means hockey
    Mona luckawiki means love
    A moonlit ice rink means
    romance with my baby
    and the stars above.

    Chorus:
    Kiki Hockey, Waikiki Hockey!
    Kiki Hockey, Waikiki Hockey!

The Hamilton Tigers (the Hockey Team, Not the Football Team)

There are probably only a handful of people alive today who can remember a time when the city of Hamilton played host to an NHL franchise. From 1920 to 1925, names like Joe Malone, Percy LeSueur, Billy Burch and Goldie Prodgers graced the Abso-Pure Ice Arena in downtown Hamilton, thrilling the nearly 4000 spectators (a decent number in those days) who came out to see their team play. Although the team never won a Stanley Cup, people in the city were just happy to have NHL-quality hockey to watch.

Hamilton tried to secure a franchise for the NHL's inaugural season of 1917–18 after the Montréal Wanderers' arena had burnt down, but Wanderers owner Sam Lichtenhein did not want to make the move, choosing instead to scrap the franchise altogether. Hamilton finally got its franchise when the Québec Bulldogs folded and were quickly bought by the Abso-Pure Ice Company for the low price of $5000. That money brought a hockey team to the city, but it had inherited a club that had only won four games in the previous season. Despite obtaining goal-scoring legends like Billy Burch and Joe Malone, the Tigers could not find a way to win hockey games. For four straight seasons, the Tigers never won more than 10 games out of the 24 played each season and naturally missed the playoffs every single year. Even the now-legendary Art Ross was brought in to coach the struggling franchise for the

1922–23 season, but little changed on the ice. The club's fortunes began to turn when two newcomers were added to the lineup.

Brothers Shorty and Red Green had been amateur stars in Sudbury and were lured over to the NHL by the Tigers for the start of the 1924–25 season. In an era when a team's starting players remained on the ice for most of the game, having players familiar with each other made all the difference in the quality of hockey, and as a result, the Tigers started to win hockey games. Along with linemates Billy Burch, the Green brothers helped to propel the Tigers from last place the year before to the best team in the league, ending up ahead of powerhouse franchises like the Montréal Canadiens, who boasted superstar Howie Morenz, and the Toronto Maple Leafs, who had the league's leading scorer Babe Dye. Going into the playoffs, it seemed as though the Tigers had their first legitimate shot at winning the Stanley Cup, but on March 9, 1925, everything changed.

On that day, the Tigers players got together and confronted owner Percy Thompson, demanding that they be paid an extra $200 for playing in the post-season. The players had a genuine reason to feel like they were not being compensated properly as the league had expanded for the first time that year, adding another team in Montréal and a team in Boston. With six teams instead of four, the season was extended from 24 to 30 games, and the players believed they should be paid accordingly for the extra work. While other teams had received bonuses and raises, Hamilton did not. League president Frank Calder was not sympathetic to the players' complaints and threatened to suspend or fine them if they did not meet their contractual obligations.

The players decided they would rather quit hockey than be taken advantage of, and without any chance of an agreement, Hamilton was disqualified from the NHL finals. The Montréal Canadiens took the Tigers place in the Stanley Cup finals against the Victoria Cougars, but they were no match for the Pacific Coast team, losing the best-of-five series three games to one. At the end of the season with no players remaining on their roster, the Tigers owners were more than happy to sell the franchise. The Hamilton Tigers moved south of the border and became the New York Americans.

The NHL has yet to return to Hamilton (though not for lack of effort), but there is still hope among the populace and especially for those aging few who once witnessed professional hockey in Steel Town.

One-eyed McGee

Frank McGee was the greatest hockey player of his generation and the offensive cornerstone of the famed Ottawa Silver Seven. He was known as an incredibly fast skater and a superior puck handler, two talents important in an era when forward passing wasn't allowed. It was these skills that helped him achieve one of the most incredible and unbreakable records in the history of hockey—he scored 14 goals in a single Stanley Cup game in 1905. Although he played just 45 official games in his hockey career, he scored 93 goals in that brief time. These heroic feats of athleticism are made even more incredible when you consider that he accomplished everything with vision in only one eye.

Playing for the Ottawa club around 1900, McGee's team rolled into Hawkesbury to play the town's best team in a charity match. The game started out friendly enough, but as things tended to in hockey games those days, the match quickly turned violent. One of the toughest and most violent players on the ice for Hawkesbury was a thug named Pokey Leahy, and he made it his job to stop McGee in any way possible. At just 5-foot-6, McGee was by far one of the smaller players on the ice, but he could check and defend himself if need be. On one play, Leahy rammed him hard into the boards, and as McGee was falling to the ice, Leahy's stick came up and caught McGee in the eye, leaving a pool of blood hardening on the ice. McGee ended up losing sight in one eye. Despite his injury and the protests of his family, McGee returned to the game he loved and went on to become one of its most legendary stars.

Six years after the incident, McGee's Ottawa Silver Seven played a game against the Montréal Wanderers, and Pokey Leahy just happened to be on their roster. As the two teams skated on the ice before the start of the game, McGee approached Leahy and told him he was going to settle the feud once and for all, to which (according to legend)

Leahy responded, "Go ahead Frankie, and I'll knock your other eye out!" Being such a small man, it didn't seem possible that McGee would be able to harm the much larger Leahy, but in the game, McGee hit him with such a hard check that Leahy went crashing down and had to be carried off the ice, never to play hockey again.

After retiring from hockey in 1906, Frank McGee enlisted with the Canadian military and joined the Commonwealth's fight in World War I. Tragically, he lost his life in the Battle of the Somme on September 16, 1916.

The End of the Senators

Since the beginning of organized hockey, Ottawa had always had one of the most successful hockey teams in history. Founded in 1883, the franchise has been known as the Ottawa Hockey Club and the Ottawa Silver Seven before finally settling on the Ottawa Senators. Prior to the formation of the NHL, the club had already amassed several Stanley Cup championships and attracted the best talent from across the country. By the time the National Hockey League was established in 1917, the franchise's success continued with four more Stanley Cup championships and countless individual awards for the players on the team. But as the league began to expand into the United States, and cities like Montréal and Toronto grew in size, Ottawa became the league's smallest market. Despite the team's success on the ice, every year was a financial struggle, and owner Frank Ahearn had been absorbing the team's losses for several years—but things were about to get much worse.

In 1929, when the stock market crashed and the world was sent into the Great Depression, it became even harder for a small-market team like Ottawa to survive. Even the larger franchises of Montréal and Toronto were operating on thin budgets. The Senators were forced to go into survival mode, and that meant selling off many of their more expensive, and therefore talented, players. Prior to the start of the 1930–31 season, the financial woes forced the Senators into a trade that no one thought would ever happen.

When it was announced that the Toronto Maple Leafs had purchased King Clancy from the Senators for $35,000, the magnitude of the deal can only be compared in modern terms to the Pittsburgh Penguins selling Sidney Crosby for cash. Despite selling off one of their most valuable and popular assets, the team could still not pull itself out of its financial woes.

The Senators' growing debts forced the team to request a one-year absence from the league for the 1931–32 season. Ottawa's players were distributed around the league. When they returned for the 1932–33 season, the team just wasn't the same anymore. With financial uncertainty, waning fan support and a distracted team, the Senators posted two consecutive losing seasons and looked on the brink of collapse. On March 15, 1934, the Ottawa Senators played their last game on home ice in a 3–2 defeat at the hands of the New York Americans. The once proud and shining example of professional hockey packed its bags and headed south for its new home in the state of Missouri, where they became the St. Louis Eagles. The Eagles themselves only lasted one year in the league before the franchise folded for good. It took 58 years before the nation's capital saw NHL hockey again.

The Return of the Senators

After 50 years, nine Stanley Cups and countless hockey legends who were destined for the Hockey Hall of Fame, the Ottawa Senators franchise had certainly left its mark on professional hockey and on the capital region. However, when the franchise folded, Ottawa still remained a hockey hub, with many junior clubs and senior teams giving the hockey-hungry citizens something to cheer for. But the city yearned for those old glory days of the Ottawa Senators' NHL-brand of hockey.

It took 50 years until Ottawa businessman and hockey aficionado Bruce Firestone, along with friends Randy Sexton and Cyril Leeder, revived the idea of bringing an NHL team back to the city. It required a lot of work on their part and a lot of financing, but the new-age Ottawa Senators were granted their franchise and returned to NHL action for the 1992–93 season.

The first few years were tough going for the expansion franchise, but the loyal hockey fans in the capital stuck by their team, and the loyalty began to pay off by the late 1990s. Young players such as Daniel Alfredsson, Marian Hossa and Jason Spezza evolved with the club and turned the losing franchise into a competitive one. The Senators had some success in the regular seasons between 1996 and 2004, but they always seemed to fall apart in the playoffs. It wasn't until 2007 that the Senators finally made it back in the Stanley Cup finals for the first time since Ottawa did it in 1927, over 80 years ago. The Sens, unfortunately, lost the series in five games to the Anaheim Ducks and have not made it back to the Cup finals since.

Proud Ontario Boy

Born in Kincardine, Paul Henderson grew up, like most Canadian boys, with dreams of making to the NHL, but he never thought that one day he would be responsible for one of the most memorable moments in hockey history.

As a Toronto Maple Leaf, Paul Henderson was a gifted player but never a top scorer like his contemporaries Phil Esposito or Guy Lafleur. He was a hard-checking, hard-working forward who got most of his goals standing in front of the net and paying the price for each and every one of them. So when he was added to Team Canada for the 1972 Summit Series versus the Soviet Red Army, he was a little surprised to be included but more than happy to have the chance.

Canadians always think of themselves as the best hockey players in the world. To most, it was a given that Canada was the best because, after all, we invented the sport. However, behind the iron curtain of communism in the frozen lands of Soviet Russia, a team of unknowns was making in-roads into the Canadians' title as the world's best hockey players. The Soviets had won several world championships before 1972 and already had several gold medals from Olympic tournaments, but at these tournaments, Canada sent its amateurs only. When the opportunity came along to have the best of the NHL take on the "amateur" talent of the Soviet Union, Canadian media predicted that the eight-game series would end in a sweep for the talent-filled Canadian roster. The Soviets were from a different world and were most certainly not expected to give Canada's best players a run for their money.

What Canada expected and what Canada got were two different things altogether. The series remained tied after a long, hard-fought battle and came down to the final game. The game itself came down to the final minutes. With just a few moments remaining in the game, Paul Henderson stepped onto the ice. Legendary radio and television broadcaster Foster Hewitt called the final moments as millions of people across Canada remained stuck in a state of tension:

A cleared pass on the far side. Liapkin rolled one to Savard. Savard clears a pass to Stapleton. He cleared the open wing to Cournoyer. Here's a shot! Henderson made a wild stab for it and fell. Here's another shot, right in front...They score! Henderson scores for Canada! And the fans and the team are going wild! Henderson, right in front of the Soviet goal with 34 seconds left in the game!

Paul Henderson, the boy from rural Ontario, went from just wanting to make the NHL to scoring arguably the most important goal in Canadian history. "I talk about the goal at least 300 days a year," Henderson likes to admit.

Walk Like an Egyptian

Coaches have tried a million-and-one ways to motivate their players to perform at their very best. Red Kelly, former Maple Leafs star player, turned coach for the team in 1976 and came up against a team of highly unmotivated players. Kelly's solution to getting the team up to snuff was a little unorthodox, to say the least.

Shortly before the start of the playoffs, Kelly came across a magazine article detailing the mystic and cosmic powers of the great pyramids of Egypt. The article left an enduring impression on the Leafs coach, who decided to try to muster that paranormal energy to help the team in its upcoming Stanley Cup run.

Kelly was never one to do things halfway. Instead of buying a few souvenir-size pyramids that fit into the palm of his hand, he had a large pyramid assembled and hung it from the ceiling of the Leafs dressing room in an effort to harness whatever spiritual powers the pyramids might be able to impart. Kelly then took his obsession one step further and placed smaller pyramids beneath the players' bench. His theory was that the cosmic energy of the pyramid would flow through the players in both the dressing room and during the game.

Darryl Sittler was the first Leafs to embrace the coach's groovy 1970s notion, and the results were immediate. The Leafs forward promptly scored five goals in his next game in an 8–3 victory over the Philadelphia Flyers in the opening round of the 1976 Stanley Cup playoffs. The rest of the team quickly jumped on the bandwagon, jockeying with one another for the seats on the players' bench closest to the pyramids. However, the power of the pyramids proved elusive for the rest of the team as the Leafs fell to the Flyers in seven games. The pyramids were never seen in Maple Leaf Gardens again.

Are You Ready to Rumble?

Ask people to guess what team they think was most likely to be involved in a record-setting game with the most penalty minutes handed out, and they would probably say the Philadelphia Flyers—and they would be right! As the history of the once nicknamed "Broad Street Bullies" has shown, they have always been a physical team and have been the home to some of the toughest players in hockey history, such as Dave "The Hammer" Schultz and the most penalized goaltender in history, Ron Hextall. However, most people would never guess that the Ottawa Senators were the Flyers' accomplices in a game in which 419 penalty minutes were handed out.

The fight-filled match occurred on March 5, 2004. This time, it wasn't just the regular tough guys on both teams who got involved in the melee. Even the normally timid goal scorers, like Flyers forward Simon Gagne and Senators centreman Daniel Alfredsson, participated in the fisticuffs. One after another, the fights just kept erupting all over the ice. At one point, before the puck was even dropped on a faceoff, a fight started. It was so bad that it seemed as though the referees were beginning to lose track of the players they had handed out penalties to.

Do You Remember the Ottawa Nationals and the Toronto Toros?

The NHL is the undisputed professional hockey league in North America. From 1917 to the present day, the league has been the home to the world's best hockey. It is the home of the "Holy Grail," the Stanley Cup, and the greatest players in the history of the sport have graced the arenas of NHL teams and will continue to do so for years to come. Despite the history and legacy of the NHL, however, rival professional leagues have popped up through the years and have tried to steal some of the glory. When the NHL first started out, it had to contend with the Pacific Coast Hockey Association (PCHA) and then the Western Hockey League (WHL). Both the PCHA and the WHL ended up folding, and for decades, the NHL was the only professional elite league in North America. Then in 1972, the World Hockey Association (WHA) arrived on the scene and genuinely challenged the league's supremacy on this continent.

The founders of the WHA wanted to capitalize on the lack of hockey teams in major cities across North America that they felt were being neglected by the NHL's refusal to pursue rapid expansion. Some of the 12 original teams to start in the WHA were the Chicago Cougars, the Minnesota Fighting Saints, the Winnipeg Jets, the Los Angeles Sharks, the Québec Nordiques and the Ottawa Nationals.

Ottawa had not seen professional hockey since the Senators folded in 1934, and it was hoped that the city's once-held passion for hockey would reignite with the arrival of the Nationals. It was expected that the approximately 9000-seat Ottawa Civic Centre would be sufficient to meet the public demand for tickets, but on a nightly basis, the club barely pulled in 4000 fans. Despite finishing with a winning record and a spot in the WHA playoffs, the Ottawa Nationals were a complete bust. Rather than trying to establish a presence in the city, the Nationals owners decided to pack up the team and sell it to the highest bidder. For the 1973–74 season, the Ottawa Nationals became the Toronto Toros.

The move was a positive one for the franchise and for the WHA because the Toros proved they could compete with the NHL's Toronto Maple Leafs. They even managed to negotiate a lease from the Maple Leafs to play in Maple Leaf Gardens after starting out at the smaller, less-centralized Varsity Arena, making it easier for fans to connect with the club. After two seasons in the city, the Toros were managing to pull in 10,000 spectators each game. Helping to attract the fans were a few former Leafs players nearing the ends of their careers but still able to play the game with skill. Frank Mahovlich joined the team in 1974, scoring 38 goals in 73 games, and 1972 Summit Series hero Paul Henderson came in and contributed 30 goals in 58 games. With those kind of numbers, the Toros finished the WHA season with the league's fifth best record but were unfortunately knocked out of the first round of the playoffs.

The good times did not last. Paying the high players' salaries and the over-market rental price for Maple Leaf Gardens meant the Toros were hemorrhaging money. It didn't help that the team finished the 1975–76 season with a losing record of 24–52–5. With the poor record came bad attendance numbers, and during the off-season, it was decided once again that the franchise would be moved to another city. This time, the Toros became the Birmingham Bulls.

The Scarborough President

The 2000 U.S. presidential election was one of the closest in American history and one of the most hotly disputed. Although former Texas governor George W. Bush lost the popular vote to Al Gore, he won the most Electoral College votes after a controversial recount in the state of Florida. In Ohio, the result was not as close, but it is worth noting because a native of Scarborough received 12 votes in his bid for the most powerful job in the world.

Ron Tugnutt was the goaltender for the Columbus Blue Jackets from 2000 to 2002. The veteran netminder had played on several NHL teams throughout his career and was picked up by the Jackets in 2000 during the expansion draft. Seven games into the 2000–01 season, Tugnutt racked up an impressive .945 save percentage and a record of 5–1–1. The Columbus Blue Jackets' marketing department decided to use Tugnutt's stellar play to their advantage and began a mock "Tugnutt for President" campaign to get the team some media coverage. Although Tugnutt was Canadian and not technically on the presidential ballot, it didn't stop some hardcore hockey fans from taking the Jackets' message to heart. To the Ohio electoral officers' surprise, they counted out 12 votes for presidential hopeful Ron Tugnutt.

Unfortunately, the veteran goalie did not win the presidency nor was he able to take his team to the Stanley Cup finals.

Famous Ontario-born Hockey Players

According to Hockey-Reference.com, 2056 players (as of the 2010–11 season) who were born in Ontario have played or are currently playing in the NHL. Below is a random sampling of those players both current and retired:

Barrie: Steve Chiasson
Belleville: Brett Hull
Brantford: Wayne Gretzky
Dryden: Chris Pronger
Fort William: Jack Adams
Kitchener: Woody Dumart, Darryl Sittler
Lindsay: Joe Primeau
London: Jeff Carter
Markham: Steven Stamkos
Mimico: Brendan Shanahan
Mitchell: Howie Morenz
Moose Factory: Jonathan Cheechoo
Naughton: Art Ross
Newton Robinson: Bob Pulford
Ottawa: King Clancy, Denis Potvin
Parry Sound: Bobby Orr
Petrolia: the Hunter brothers (Dale, Dave and Mark)
Plattsville: Babe Siebert
Renfrew: Jim Peplinski
Scarborough: Rick Tocchet
Skead: George Armstrong
St. Catherines: Brian Bellows
Thunder Bay: the Staal brothers (Eric, Jordan and Marc)

Toronto: P.K. Subban
Welland: Nathan Horton
Weston: Paul Coffey
Winchester: Larry Robinson

Ontario Hockey Quick Facts

- On March 23, 1918, Toronto Arenas forward Alf Skinner scored the first hat-trick (though it wasn't called a "hat-trick" yet) by an NHL player in the Stanley Cup finals. Sadly, his heroics were in vain as the Arenas ended up losing the game 6–4 to the Vancouver Millionaires. They did, however, end up winning the Stanley Cup.

- In the first two games of NHL history in 1917, the Montréal Canadiens beat the Ottawa Senators 7–4 and the Montréal Wanderers beat the Toronto Arenas 10–9.

- While Montréal Canadiens goalie Georges Vézina was the first goaltender to record a shutout during the NHL's inaugural season in 1917, Ottawa Senators goalie Clint Benedict was the first to record two shutouts, which he did the following season.

- The Ontario Hockey League was formed in 1974 and consisted of 20 teams. Three of those teams were from the United States: Erie Otters (Pennsylvania), Plymouth Whalers (Michigan) and Saginaw Spirit (Michigan).

- Ottawa hockey legend Frank McGee was the nephew of Thomas D'Arcy McGee, one of

Canada's Fathers of Confederation and the only Canadian victim of a political assassination at the federal level.

- Centre Laurie Boschman was the first captain of the modern Ottawa Senators, in 1992.
- The Toronto Maple Leafs became the first NHL franchise to win three straight Stanley Cups, with victories in 1947, 1948 and 1949.
- Since their last Stanley Cup championship in 1967, the Toronto Maple Leafs have not made it back to the Stanley Cup finals.
- In a game between the Toronto Maple Leafs and the Ottawa Senators, Leafs forward Ken Doraty became the only player in NHL history to score a hat-trick in overtime as the Leafs won 7–4. In those days, the overtime period was a mandatory 10-minute period and not sudden death like it is today.
- Ottawa Senators goalie Alex Connell became the first goaltender to win 30 games in a season when the Sens beat the Montréal Canadiens 3–2 in the final game of the 1926–27 season.
- The Toronto Maple Leafs' current home is the Air Canada Centre (ACC). Construction began in February 1997 and the first hockey game was held on February 20, 1999, against the Montréal Canadiens. The ACC's seating capacity for hockey games is 18,800 and is located in the heart of the city, close to the CN Tower, the

theatre district, restaurants, 15 major hotels, shopping and two main transportation arteries: the Gardiner Expressway and Union Station (which services the Toronto Transit Commission and GO Transit system).

- Toronto Maple Leafs star Syl Apps was also a member of Canada's pole-vault team at the 1936 Summer Olympics in Berlin, Germany. He came in sixth place overall in his event.
- Gordie Howe played some junior league hockey in Galt.

Chapter Two

Are You Ready for Some Football?

The best thing about these games, there's no Russians or Swedes playing.

–Don Cherry

The Cup

Canada's governor generals love to support Canadian athletic endeavours. Lord Stanley created the Stanley Cup in 1893 in support of Canadian hockey, and in 1909, governor general Lord Albert Grey donated the Grey Cup to recognize Canadian football. However, when the University of Toronto Varsity Blues won the first Grey Cup game on December 4, 1909, the Cup had not even been made yet. Lord Grey only presented the completed Cup to the winners three months after the actual game.

No, the Tigers Won the First Cup

As you just read, the University of Toronto Varsity Blues were the first recipients of the Grey Cup in 1909. However, if you were to take a look at the original bowl of the Grey Cup, you would see that the Hamilton Tiger Seniors are listed as the 1908 champions.

The reason for this erratum occurred when the Varsity Blues won the Cup in 1912 and 1913 and felt they had the right to hold onto the trophy until someone else defeated them in a Grey Cup game. The Hamilton Tiger Seniors objected to the Varsity Blues' hoarding of the Cup, and when they finally won it in 1915, they decided to get even with their Toronto rivals. They felt their best revenge was to rewrite history.

As is the tradition with the Cup, the winning team gets to have the team name engraved on the trophy, but instead of putting themselves as the 1915 winners, the Tigers had the engraver put them as the 1908 winners. This date, of course, was impossible because the Cup had not yet been created in 1908, but the damage had been done.

The Rough Riders

No, not Saskatchewan. That's right, the Ottawa Rough Riders. Although many former fans like to forget their old team, there was a time when the "Black and Red" from the nation's capital were one of the top teams in the Canadian Football League (CFL).

One of the oldest and longest-lived franchises in professional sports, the Ottawa Rough Riders were founded in 1876, when they were known as the Ottawa Football Club. They officially adopted the name Rough Riders in 1898 (though they were also known as the Ottawa Senators from 1925 to 1930, changing back to Rough Riders in 1931). The club's first championship season came in 1898, when they beat the Toronto Varsity Blues in the Canadian championship. Over the next few years, the Ottawa Rough Riders and Ottawa College shared the Canadian championship title between them, with the Riders winning in 1900 and 1902 and Ottawa College in 1901. At the time, there were several football leagues operating in Canada, such as the Québec League, the Ottawa City League and the Ontario League, just to name a few. The Rough Riders switched leagues several times in their history before the formation of the CFL in 1958.

After their championship runs in the early part of the century, the Rough Riders began a steep decline, attributing the loss of players to the more lucrative hockey clubs that had begun to spring up all over the area in pursuit of the Stanley Cup. For about 20 years, the Ottawa Rough Riders were one of the worst football clubs in Canada and were always on the verge of going bankrupt (a familiar theme in Ottawa's sports history).

During their slide, another local Ottawa team was on the rise. The Ottawa St. Brigids were developing top talent of their own but managed to hold onto their players. In 1923, in desperate need of help, the Rough Riders merged with the St. Brigids and ushered in a new era of success and prosperity for the still-named Ottawa Rough Riders.

Completely turned around, the team won the Grey Cup in 1925 and 1926 while known as the Ottawa Senators. In 1925, the club defeated three-time defending champion powerhouse Queen's, then beat Winnipeg for the championship, and in 1926, they defeated old rivals Toronto Varsity.

However, what goes up must come down. The following season, after their 1926 Grey Cup, they began to lose games en masse. Again another local Ottawa team, this time the Ottawa Rangers, were developing quality talent of their own and enjoying success out on the field, so the Riders absorbed them in 1933. This absorption did not take immediate effect as it was still another seven years before the team won the Grey Cup in 1940.

Several teams went out of existence during World War II, but the Riders—along with the Toronto Argonauts, Toronto's Balmy Beach Beachers and Montréal—formed the Eastern Rugby Football Union and continued playing ball. The Riders won the 1942 title, the only one during the Union's brief existence. When the war ended, sporting life thankfully returned to normal.

Two Teams, One Name

For much of the Ottawa Rough Riders history, there was a team in Saskatchewan with the same name. Over the history of the two teams, this has confused many and has led to much ridicule from our neighbours to the south who laugh at how a league with under 10 teams could have two teams with the same name (although Saskatchewan spells it "Roughriders" and Ottawa was the "Rough Riders"). The reason for the double name was that the Saskatchewan Roughriders had existed since 1910, and when the CFL was formed in 1958, both clubs were allowed to keep their respective names.

The two clubs met at the 1951 Grey Cup for the first time. The Ottawa Rough Riders came out victorious to win their fourth title. But again, after another Grey Cup victory, the team went into a decline. They resurfaced in 1960 for the start of a new dynasty that lasted two decades.

Under the guidance of head coach Frank Clair and along with key players like Russ Jackson, Whit Tucker, Tom Clements and Tony Gabriel, the Riders were one of the CFL's best teams, winning the Grey Cup five times in two decades (1960, 1968, 1969, 1973 and 1976).

Throughout the 1980s and '90s, the Riders were an average team and never managed a return to the Grey Cup after their 1981 loss to the Edmonton Eskimos. Because of dwindling fan support, poor ownership and an accumulation of losing seasons, the bottom eventually fell out on the club in 1996, when they folded operations for good.

Professional football did return to Ottawa in 2002 when a new franchise named the Renegades joined the CFL, but a string of losing seasons and poor attendance once again sunk football in the nation's capital in 2006. However, in 2010, it was announced that the CFL would return to Ottawa in 2013 when the Ottawa Sports and Entertainment Group revealed their plans to rejuvenate Lansdowne Park and bring football back to the hungry fans. The name of the team, however, remains up in the air. Many fans and the owner of the new franchise, Jeff Hunt, would like to see the return of the Rough Riders name, but the naming rights remain in the hands of the Saskatchewan Roughriders since they've had the name the longest.

Ottawa Rough Riders Retired Numbers
11—Ron Stewart
12—Russ Jackson
26—Whit Tucker
40—Bruno Bitkowski
60—Jim Coode
62—Moe Racine
70—Bobby Simpson
71—Gerry Organ
72—Tony Golab
77—Tony Gabriel

The Miracle of the Cup

From 1945 to 1947, the Toronto Argonauts won three consecutive Grey Cup championships. For those three years, employees at the Argos head office enjoyed the unique privilege of getting to look at the Grey Cup every day, mounted on a shelf in the main lobby for everyone to see. However, the Cup was almost lost when a huge fire broke out in 1947. The fire destroyed almost everything in the offices: furniture, paintings and trophies. In fact, everything was lost except the Cup.

During the fire, the Grey Cup fell from its perch on the top shelf, but instead of plummeting into the fiery abyss like everything else, one of the Cup's handles hooked onto a nail. Suspended off the floor, it avoided the fire below and was also separated from the burning wall. When firefighters entered the offices, everything was burnt except for the Grey Cup, hanging neatly on the wall. With the application of a little elbow grease and polish, the Cup was ready to be handed out again for the next season.

The Infamous Tripper

The day after the 1957 Grey Cup between the Hamilton Tiger-Cats and the Winnipeg Blue Bombers, people were not talking about the fact that the Cats completely mauled the Bombers by a final score of 32–7, but about one play in particular that left spectators and announcers scratching their heads in disbelief.

Late in the fourth quarter, with Hamilton way out in the lead at 25–0, Ray Bawel, a Tiger-Cats defensive back, intercepted a Blue Bomber pass and began running unimpeded down the sideline toward a sure touchdown. In those days, fans could purchase field seats that put them into the thick of the action on the field but also dangerously close to the players. All of a sudden, out of the crowd of spectators, a foot appeared and caught Bawel unaware, sending him face-first into the muddy turf. The stadium suddenly fell quiet. Bawel bounced to his feet and began screaming at the offending fan. By the time most people realized what had happened, the guilty fan had quietly blended back into the crowd. For the longest time, no one could figure out who the mysterious fan was, having only grainy images of a man dressed in a trench coat wearing a black Ivy-league cap.

After some investigation, the media finally got wind that the tripper was prominent Toronto lawyer David Humpfrey, who would later go on to become Justice Humpfrey of the Ontario Court. As to the alleged tripping incident, Humpfrey told a different story. During the course of the game, the lawyer ran into a man who had been a jury foreman in a criminal proceeding in which Humpfrey had represented the accused. Humpfrey lost the case, and his client was sentenced to death for his crimes. Humpfrey blamed the jury foreman for leading the decision to fall in the defendant's favour, so when he saw the man at the game that day, he lost his temper and tried to get at the man and, in the process, ended up tripping the Tiger-Cats player.

Fortunately, the incident did not end up altering the outcome of the game as Bawel was named most outstanding player of the game and the Ti-Cats won the Cup. Two months after the game, Bawel received a package at his home in Evansville, Indiana, and inside was a gold watch with an inscription that read, "From the Tripper, Grey Cup 1957."

Dick Shatto

All-purpose back Dick Shatto is one of the Argonauts' all-time greats. In 12 years with the Argonauts, he retired with more touchdowns and more offensive yards than any Argo before him. However, during his career with the Argos and his 30 years playing and coaching, he never won a Grey Cup.

Doug Flutie Joins the Argos

Standing a mere 5-foot-8, Manchester, Maryland-born Doug Flutie did not have much hope in cracking a major NFL lineup as a starting quarterback. Football was a game of giants, and a quarterback had to be as tall as or above the fray on the field to spot his passes. Despite his height hindrance, Flutie was given a chance in the NFL because of his sheer talent and intelligence with the ball. After all, college football didn't name him the 1984 Heisman Trophy winner for nothing. He played one season with the Chicago Bears and another with the New England Patriots but with little success. He was a small man in a big-minded American game. So in 1990, he signed with the CFL's BC Lions.

The Canadian game was the perfect fit for Flutie's style of football. It was dynamic, fast paced and forced players to rely more on skill and less on size. His first year with the Lions was not overly successful, but the Canadian game was something completely new to him. After that first season, he never looked back and became one of the most dominant players in league history. In 1992, the Calgary Stampeders offered him a load of money, and Flutie promptly led the team to the Grey Cup championship. After three more seasons in Calgary, Flutie jumped ship and landed in Toronto with the Argonauts.

After their thrilling 1991 Grey Cup championship, the Argonauts fell into a prolonged slump. Even the addition of Wayne Gretzky to the management group could not turn the fortunes of the club around, and season after season, they sank farther into the mire of the league's lesser teams. In 1996, sensing the team needed a change, Toronto Blue Jays vice president Paul Veeston was named as the Argos new president, coach Don Matthews was brought back as coach, and most importantly, Doug Flutie was named the team's new starting quarterback. Flutie led the Argos to a 15–3–0 season and secured a berth in the Grey Cup Championship against the Edmonton Eskimos. Through a blizzard of snow and wind at Hamilton's Ivor Wayne Stadium, Flutie guided the team to an exciting 43–37 win over the Eskimos. Flutie did the same thing the following year, taking the team into the playoffs with a self-same 15–3–0 record and beat up the Saskatchewan Roughriders 47–23 en route to his second straight Grey Cup championship.

In just eight seasons in the CFL, Doug Flutie had nearly rewritten the record book. He won six regular-season MVP awards and was MVP in all three of his Grey Cup championships. He threw for 41,355 yards and 270 career touchdowns, and in 2007, he became the first American-born athlete to be entered into the Canadian Football Hall of Fame. Naturally, with numbers like those, the NFL decided to take another look at Doug Flutie, and he left the Argos to join the Buffalo Bills in 1998. But he never forgot about the place that made him feel at home. Flutie spoke of those feelings at the 2007 Hall of Fame induction ceremony.

"I feel accepted. A lot of people in the States thought I was Canadian, the way I waved the flag for Canada. Part of that is that I really appreciated the support I got up here from the fans. I was never second-guessed up here. The height thing...whenever I was playing in the States I had a chip on my shoulder. But up here I just had fun."

Fog Bowl

During the 1962 Grey Cup at Toronto's Canadian National Exhibition (CNE) Stadium between the Hamilton Tiger-Cats and the Winnipeg Blue Bombers, an unseasonable warm spell caused a dense fog to roll in off Lake Ontario and slowly envelop the field to the point that broadcasters and fans alike could not see what was happening on the field.

At first when the game started, it was a light fog hovering in the stadium, but as the game wore on, it swept across the stadium like a ghost blanketing the field in white mist. The players and coaches at field level could make out just enough to continue playing, but for the fans at home and in the stands, it became impossible to follow. American TV broadcaster Jim McKay was calling the game and sarcastically mocked the play on the field. "This is the greatest football spectacle of them all. I've not seen hitting as hard as this in any game...what a pity the fog had to spoil it."

By the third quarter of the game, fans who had paid good money to see a Grey Cup celebration were getting impatient. Shouting matches between the fans erupted in the stands and the police had to be called in to break up fights between the Winnipeg and Hamilton supporters. This left CFL commissioner G. Sydney Halter with the tough decision on whether to suspend the game or allow it to continue to the annoyance of the viewing audiences. After consulting with the National Weather Service, Halter suspended the game with only 10 minutes remaining and resumed it the next day. At that juncture, Winnipeg was up by a single point.

In the history of the Grey Cup, teams have had to play through bone-chilling cold, snow storms, sleet and muddied fields, but never before had a game been suspended until a harmless fog rolled into the Big Smoke. When the game restarted the next afternoon, it was a beautiful clear day, but only 15,000 of the original 32,000 fans showed up to watch the final 10 minutes of the game. The remaining fans watched as nothing changed from the previous day, and the Blue Bombers held onto their one-point lead to win the Grey Cup by a final score of 28–27.

The Canadian Football Hall of Fame

Although the city of Hamilton won the rights to be the hosts of the Canadian Football Hall of Fame in 1962, it wasn't until 1972 that it officially opened to the public. When the Hall was scheduled to open in 1962, the curators had barely finished putting the artifacts on the shelves when the land and the building it was housed in were sold to the Ontario Ministry of Education, and the Hall of Fame was forced into limbo.

For the next 10 years, the CFL looked for a new home but could not agree on a site. Then in 1968, the city found a new location next to city hall. Construction on the new Hall of Fame began in earnest. By 1972, with construction complete, the Canadian Football Hall of Fame opened on the same day that the city hosted the Grey Cup.

The Day the Cup Disappeared

The Grey Cup is a priceless piece of Canadian history, and it is for that reason that thieves stole it from a display case in the offices of the Ottawa Rough Riders in 1969. On December 20, several brazen thieves broke into the Rough Riders offices at Lansdowne Park and stole the Grey Cup with relative ease. The next day, the police department received a ransom letter demanding an undisclosed, yet allegedly exorbitant, amount of money for the

Cup's safe return. When league officials learned of the ransom demands, they laughed at the amount and told police to tell the thieves that they could keep the trophy. CFL officials were confident that, given a little time, the thieves wouldn't know what to do with the Cup and eventually it would find its way back to the rightful owners.

Well, they called the thieves' bluff perfectly, and a few weeks later, Toronto police received an anonymous call directing them to a phone booth on the corner of Dundas and Parliament. Once there, the police found a key in the phone's change slot that led them to a locker in Union Station's rail terminal. Inside the locker, police recovered the original Grey Cup, completely undamaged.

The thieves were never caught. Since that incident, a $550 replica now makes its rounds in the CFL while the original Grey Cup is safe behind glass at the Canadian Football Hall of Fame.

Thy Will Be Done

Sometimes, all it takes is a few flippant words to the wrong deity to completely change the outcome of a game. It is usually the coach's job to rally his team with inspiring words in the face of overwhelming odds. However, during the 1969 Grey Cup semi-finals, Ottawa Rough Riders head coach Frank Clair—after losing the first game of a two-game, total-points series by a score of 22–14 to the Toronto Argonauts—didn't have to say a word after he got all the help he needed from Argos coach Leo

Cahill, who famously said these words: "It will take an Act of God to beat the Argos."

Well, it seemed God was listening that day and did not want to disappoint Cahill. Ottawa came back in the second game to crush the Argos 32–3 to win the series by an aggregate score of 46–25. The Ottawa Rough Riders and their fans thanked Cahill and the Lord above for His assistance as they went on to beat the Saskatchewan Roughriders to win the Grey Cup.

Team Songs

Hamilton Tiger-Cats Chant

Oski-wee-wee
Oski-wah-wah
Holy Mackinaw!
Tigers, eat 'em raw!
(Repeat)

Toronto Argonauts, "Go Argos Go"

Go Toronto Argos go go go
Pull together fight the foe foe foe
Scoring touchdowns for the blue on blue
The Argos will win for you.
Full of fight and courage you can't stop
They pile up the points until they reach the top
Pull together till the Grey Cup's won
Go Argos go go go
(Repeat)

A Star Is Born

During the summer of 1989 at a game between the BC Lions and the Toronto Argonauts, there was a break in play. The stadium's cameras liked to take such opportunities to scan the crowd and put people up on the Jumbotron. As the cameraman slowly panned through the crowd, he saw the usual suspects present at CFL games—fathers and sons, face-painted frat boys, dressed-up hard-core superfans—but then someone new caught the cameraman's eye. Dressed in a tight-fitting Labatt T-shirt that left absolutely nothing to the imagination, a then-unknown Pamela Anderson was enthusiastically jumping up and down and waving to the equally excited crowd.

For the rest of the game, without fail, every time there was a stoppage in play, the cameraman's electronic eye wandered back to the buxom blonde babe bouncing in the stands. A few times, the game had already resumed on the field but the camera was still firmly fixed on Anderson as she cheered on the BC Lions. As well as catching the eye of every single man in the stadium, she also caught the eye of a talent agent who was watching the game, and the rest, as they say, is history.

D-Fence?

On September 1, 1990, a game was played in which defence did not exist. CFL fans are used to high-scoring games, but no fan walking into the Toronto Argonaut–BC Lions game at the Skydome that night expected to witness a record being set. Both quarterbacks were on fire that day as they picked apart the other team's defensive line, but it was Argos quarterback Matt Dunigan who came out on top, leading his team to a 68–43 dismantling of the Lions.

Between the two teams, the total number of points scored was 111. Amazingly, neither defensive coordinator lost their job the next day, although I'm sure they reviewed their playbooks thoroughly.

In another record, the most lopsided victory in the CFL happened on October 20, 1956, when the Montréal Alouettes, led by quarterback Sam Etcheverry, defeated the Hamilton Tiger-Cats by a score of 82–14.

Ontario Football Quick Facts

- At the 1982 Grey Cup at Toronto's CNE Stadium, fans had to deal with cold temperatures, blowing winds, pouring rain and the fact that their Toronto Argonauts were losing the game to the Edmonton Eskimos. Canadian football fans are a tough bunch and can patiently sit through all kinds of miserable weather conditions, but when the thousands of fans also had to deal with the hundreds of toilets at the stadium that suddenly started backing up, it was too much for them. The game was later dubbed the "Toilet Bowl" by the media.

- Did you know that an Academy Award–nominated actor once played for the Toronto Argonauts? Nominated for his work in the 1938 movie *Algiers*, Gene Lockhart played football for the Argos from 1910 to 1912. He is the father of actress June Lockhart, who is known for her roles in *Lassie* and *Lost in Space*.

- The Toronto Argonauts were founded in 1873 by members of the Toronto Argonaut Rowing Club, making them the third oldest existing professional sports team in North America. Only the Chicago Cubs (1870) and the Atlanta Braves (1871) are older.

- The Argonauts have won the Grey Cup a record 15 times, most recently in 2004. They have appeared in the Grey Cup final game 21 times. They've won the Grey Cup in 1914, 1921, 1933, 1937, 1938, 1945, 1946, 1947, 1950, 1952, 1983, 1991, 1996, 1997 and 2004.

- From 1958 to 2010, the regular-season record for the Argos was 395–459–12 (.463 winning percentage). The Argos are 23–25 (.478) in the playoffs since 1958.

- In their long illustrious history, the Argos have only retired four numbers:

    22—Dick Shatto (1954–65)
    31—Michael "Pinball" Clemons (1989–2000)
    55—Joe "King" Krol (1945–52)
    60—Danny Nykoluk (1957–71).

- Danny Nykoluk is the older brother of former Toronto Maple Leafs hockey player and Leafs head coach (1980–84) Mike Nykoluk. Mike was assistant coach to Fred Shero when the Philadelphia Flyers won the Stanley Cup in 1974 and 1975.

Chapter Three

More Than Just the Blue Jays

It's a Canadian Game!

Ask any American who invented the game of baseball, and they will immediately look at you like you're some sort of crazy person and say with pride, "*We* invented it, of course!" And they would have good reason to believe it. Most American books and websites will tell you that the game of baseball was invented in 1845 when Alexander Cartwright of New York drew out the lines for the first-ever baseball diamond and devised a set of written rules and regulations.

The fact is, however, that the first recorded game of baseball occurred in the town of Beachville in 1838, seven years before Cartwright had even thought of creating a baseball diamond. A detailed description of that inaugural game was provided in a letter penned by Dr. Adam E. Ford, but it was not officially published in *Sporting Life* magazine until 1886. In his letter, Ford writes as if he were a modern-day radio announcer:

> *Good afternoon, Ladies and Gentlemen, and welcome to the pasture out back of Enoch Burdick's*

> *store, here in Beachville, Ontario, for today's first recorded game of Base between the Beachville Eleven and the visitors from Zorra. Yes, this June 4th, 1838, is an exciting day. The knockers have all brought their favorite clubs along and are ready to circle those byes at blazing speed.*

Ford goes on to describe the game as having five bases, or "byes," with baselines 19 metres long, and he charts the distance between home base and the pitcher at 14 metres. Fairly and unfairly pitched balls (now called strikes and balls) were described, and techniques were delineated for how the pitcher could make it more difficult for the "knocker" to hit the ball, such as using curveballs and fastballs.

So the next time an American proudly tells you that baseball is *their* game, tell them that the sport's home is in fact north of the border, in the proud Ontario town of Beachville.

The Maple Leafs of Baseball

Among Ontario towns like Guelph, Hamilton and Toronto, competition for new business development was fierce, and a successful baseball club was just one tool that the politicians and businessmen could use to advertise their town's thriving economy and positive spirit.

The problem they had was how to field a competitive team. In the mid-1800s, baseball was not the most widely practiced sport, and while there were enough players willing to join the team, it was difficult to put together a squad that could display the proper civic pride. The original Guelph Maple Leafs team, for example, was made up from players living in Guelph who were looking for something to do after work. Everyone on the team had a regular day job: one was a miller, another a butcher, four worked in local factories and even the local Methodist clergyman decided to get involved in the game. Despite their blue collars (and, in one case, black-and-white collar), the team was a good ball club. In 1864, when they defeated their Hamilton rivals—whose lineup included several American ringers—news of their baseball prowess began to spread south of the border.

For several years, the Guelph Maple Leafs were the talk of the baseball world and continued to dominate all challengers. A reporter for the *New York Clipper* newspaper once wrote, "the Canucks are not to be trifled with, and unless better teams are pitted against them in the future, the laurels may pass from the American boys to them." The call went out to rescue America's pastime from the clutches of Canadian gloves, and it was answered by the Boston Red Stockings in the summer of 1873.

The Boston Red Stockings were one of the strongest clubs of the late 19th century. From 1872 to 1875, the Red Stockings won four consecutive National Association championships and accomplished the feat with an incredible record of 205 wins and just 50 losses. No one gave the little Canadian club from Guelph any chance of winning the match.

The game was played on the Maple Leafs home field in front of about 5000 eager fans from all the surrounding towns who witnessed a 27–8 massacre of their team by the powerful Boston Red Stockings. Many spectators, however, noticed there was something a little off about the baseballs that were being thrown whenever one of the Boston players came up to bat. One reporter even noted, "the ball seemed a great deal more lively than the dead ball generally used." Nothing was ever proven conclusively, but the public sided with the Maple Leafs, citing the impossibility of winning a game fairly by a margin of 27–8. American author Zane Grey even wrote a short story about the game entitled "The Winning Ball," in which he details the story of the cheating American baseball club and the Canadian underdogs that won the game in the end, at least in his version of the story.

KKK

About 135 years ago, society's attitudes regarding racist groups were a little bit more tolerant than they are today. Can you imagine a group like the Ku Klux Klan fielding a semi-professional, travelling baseball team today? But in 1874, the KKK had one of the better baseball teams playing at the time.

After losing the American Civil War, the extreme racists of the South formed the Ku Klux Klan to advance their white supremacist ideals. On top of lynchings, house and cross burnings, bombings and other unsavoury acts, the Klan apparently also liked to play baseball. The Oneida, New York, chapter of the

Klan did well enough during the season to make it to the 1874 World Semi-Professional Championships in Watertown, New York. Their first opponents were the Guelph Maple Leafs. The Canadian bats proved to be far more precise than those of the Ku Klux Klan, and the Canadians won the game handily, 13–4. In the end, the Maple Leafs beat out all other semi-pro teams in Canada and the United States to claim the "international" championship.

Babe Ruth in Toronto

Before he became the Babe Ruth of legend in Boston and New York, Ruth was a pitcher with the minor league Providence Grays. On September 15, 1914, Ruth and his team crossed the Canadian border to play the Toronto Maple Leafs of the International Baseball League at Toronto's Island Stadium. It was during the course of the game that Babe Ruth hit his first professional home run.

A Canadian Invention

Playing for the Providence Grays in the mid-1880s, Toronto-born Art Irwin broke two fingers when he attempted to catch a speeding baseball with his bare hands. In those days, fielders, like cricket players, did not wear gloves to catch the ball. Searching for a solution, Irwin bought an oversized buckskin glove and stuffed it with extra padding, thus giving birth to the first recognizable baseball mitt.

Canadian-brand Baseball

When the Toronto Blue Jays prepared to host their first home game on April 7, 1977, few expected that the weather would end up being the main story. Just before the start of the game as fans were packing into the open-air Exhibition Stadium, a minor snowstorm suddenly blew across the city and instantly turned the green field a cool Canadian white. In true Canadian form, the Blue Jays won the game by a score of 9–5.

Is This Wrestling?

People who do not like baseball will often complain about the "lack of action" in the game. Canadians like hockey because it's fast and has plenty of hitting. So what happens when true-blood Canadians play baseball?

Normally, when a player disagrees with an umpire's decision, he might get a little angry, get in the ump's face and throw down a few curse words. It's a rarity in this gentle game that any player would consider using violence when disagreeing over a bad call. Well, Tim Flood of the 1907 Toronto Maple Leafs was that rare player.

During the game, Flood lost his cool when he thought umpire John Conway made a bad call. Instead of contesting the judgement by talking to him, Flood simply lost his mind. He took two steps and drop-kicked Conway directly in the chest, dropping the umpire to the ground. Unfortunately for Flood, a police detective happened to be at the game and quickly arrested Flood for assaulting the umpire.

Flood's bad luck continued when he was brought before a less-than-sympathetic judge and sentenced to 15 days of hard labour for his unsportsmanlike conduct.

Fergie Jenkins

On July 21, 1991, more than a decade after retiring from professional baseball, Chatham native Ferguson Jenkins became the first Canadian inducted into the Baseball Hall of Fame in Cooperstown, New York. At the ceremony, Jenkins humbly thanked his parents and the good people of Chatham for all their support over the years.

Baseball's history in Canada is just as long as the United States', but never before had our country produced a player of Jenkins' calibre. A talented pitcher, Jenkins was known for his incredible accuracy in the strike zone and for a deceptive slider that fooled many of the greatest players of his time. In his 18-year major league career, Jenkins won 284 games, started 594 times, struck out 3192 batters and had 20 or more wins in seven seasons, all with four teams (Philadelphia Phillies, Chicago Cubs, Texas Rangers and the Boston Red Sox).

His accomplishments were not lost on his home country as he was awarded the Lou Marsh Trophy as Canada's top male athlete on four occasions, was the recipient of the Order of Canada and was the subject of a documentary produced by the National Film Board of Canada.

Growing up, though, Jenkins did not just play baseball, his 6-foot-5 frame helped him out on the basketball court (he even travelled with the Harlem Globetrotters at one point in his career), and he also loved hockey, making it as far as the Junior B affiliate of the Montréal Canadiens. But baseball was his passion. Despite growing up in such a small community, Jenkins' natural talent on the mound made up for few opportunities to play against talented opponents.

Jenkins made his major league debut with the Philadelphia Phillies in 1965, but he is best remembered for his time with the Chicago Cubs from 1967 to 1972. This time in his career culminated in his winning the 1971 Cy Young Award as the National League's premiere pitcher. Although his numbers slowly declined over the next few years, Jenkins always remained a viable starter who could be called on to work late into games. He retired after the 1983 season.

Once he was done with the majors, Jenkins continued to play ball in Ontario's amateur inter-county league. He also briefly coached for the Cubs. Although he never won a World Series, his induction into the Hall of Fame was the pinnacle of his career.

World Series in Canada, Twice!

Not many people in the U.S. thought much of Canadian baseball teams, namely the only two at the time, the Montréal Expos and the Toronto Blue Jays. The Expos joined the major leagues first, in 1969, and the Jays followed in 1977, but neither club really challenged for the World Series title until 1992, when the Jays made the run late into October.

The 1992 season saw the Blue Jays put in one of their best performances since joining the league, ending up in first place overall in the American League. This put them in a good position going into the playoffs, but as the sports cliché goes, the playoffs are a completely different season altogether.

Up first in the 1992 playoffs for the Blue Jays were the Oakland Athletics, and after going down in the first game of the series, the Jays bounced back and won the series in six games. The Jays were in the World Series for the first time, playing against the Atlanta Braves. Right from the start of the series, it was clear that our neighbours to the south were not aware of certain Canadian cultural norms when, during the singing of the national anthems in Atlanta, members of the U.S. military band raised the Canadian flag upside down.

All it would take for the Jays to make baseball history was eight days and six baseball games. For the first time in Canadian history, baseball had managed to capture the attention of the entire nation. Some 11 million Canadians tuned into some part of the six-game series, and when first baseman Joe Carter got the final out of the series, our country went wild with baseball fever. While Canada celebrated the first-ever World Series title, the city of Toronto went absolutely ballistic. Thousands of fans poured out into the streets in a civil display of pride.

Not only did the Blue Jays win one World Series, but they also managed to make the playoffs the next year, beat the Chicago White Sox in the American League championship and return to the big show for another title shot against the Philadelphia Phillies. Leading the 1993 World Series three games to two, Jays first baseman Joe Carter came to bat with one out in the bottom of the ninth inning with the White Sox leading 6–5, with Rickey Henderson and Paul Molitor on base. On a 2-2 count, Carter swung and hit a three-run home run against pitcher Mitch Williams, knocking it over the fence to win the game and the World Series. The only other player to hit a World Series–winning home run was Bill Mazeroski, who did it against the New York Yankees in 1960.

To this day, the memory of that moment remains clear for so many Canadian baseball—and even non-baseball—fans. The flash of the bat, the crowd rising to its feet, the collective holding of the breath and the final moment of relief as the ball sailed over the left-field fence. Carter watched the whole thing as he ran the bases, and once the ball cleared the fence, he began jumping in the air like a crazed child. The moment he hit home plate, he was swarmed by his teammates who raised him on their shoulders. That day, October 23, 1993, produced one of the most memorable moments in the game of baseball, one for the ages.

Not since the 1978 New York Yankees had a baseball team repeated as champions. Even more remarkable was that the Blue Jays were in just their 17th season since joining the majors. In two short years, the Blue Jays went from being "that Canadian team up north" to one of the more envied and even hated clubs in baseball, and as everyone knows in sports, when you're hated, you're good (just ask the Yankees).

Canada's Baseball Surprise

Olympic baseball, since its entry as a medal sport in 1992, has been dominated by a handful of countries that greedily hang onto their top spots. Cuba, Japan and the U.S. have consistently finished with a medal in each of the Olympics, with the Cubans leading the way with three gold medals and one silver medal. Except for the Australian baseball team at the 2004 Olympics in Athens, Greece, only one other team has been able to challenge the dominance of those three nations.

The Canadian team came out of nowhere and had already surprised everyone by simply qualifying for the Olympics. The team roster had names that many people were not familiar with, but Canadian amateur baseball fans believed that they had a good chance.

Led by second baseman Richard "Stubby" Clapp, the Canadian team strung together a bunch of wins that placed them in serious contention for a medal. In the opening game, they steamrolled over Chinese Taipei and won the game 7–0, then followed it up by decisive victories over the Italians and the Dutch. The

Canadians lost two games in a row to the superior Cuban and Japanese teams, but their record of 5–2 put them into third place. Media from Canada flocked to Greece to report on the story of this Cinderella baseball team.

The Canadians defied all odds and made it into the semi-final round against the favourite Cubans. If they could beat the Cubans, the Canadian baseball team would surely have to be mentioned in the same breath as the American Olympic hockey team of 1980 that defeated the Russians in what is now called the "Miracle on Ice." Canada kept the game close with some ace pitching and excellent defence from all corners of the field. By the eighth inning, Canada was holding onto a slim 3–2 lead. The Canadians could not hold them back forever, and the Cubans rallied with six runs late in the match, winning the game 8–5. There was a profound sense of disappointment on the Canadians' faces as the Cubans celebrated their advancement into the gold medal game.

Canada was left to battle it out for the bronze with the Japanese, who had lost to the Australians. But history was not made in that game either, as the Canadians were trounced 11–2. Canada had to settle for fourth. The Canadians did not disappoint in their run for the gold medal and, along the way, won new fans around the world and missed becoming the top story in the Olympics by a few runs.

Richard Fowler

Toronto-born Dick Fowler enjoyed a 10-year major league career with the Philadelphia Athletics in the 1940s. His career highlights include tossing a no-hitter on September 9, 1945, against the St. Louis Browns. Fowler was the first Canadian to pitch a no-hitter and did so in his first start after serving three years in the Canadian military in World War II.

Jeff Heath

Fort William native John Heath was the first player in the American League to register 20 doubles, 20 triples and 20 home runs in one season in 1941 for the Cleveland Indians. American George Brett was the only other player to ever do this in 1979.

Heath played in the majors for 14 years before retiring in 1949 with a career batting average of .293, 194 home runs and 887 runs batted in.

Toronto Blue Jays Quick Facts

- In 1990, the Toronto Blue Jays made a blockbuster move, trading Tony Fernandez and Fred McGriff to the San Diego Padres for Joe Carter and Roberto Alomar. With Carter and Alomar, the Blue Jays went on to win two World Series titles in a row, in 1992 and 1993.

- As the Blue Jays coach in 1992, Cito Gaston became the first black manager to win a World Series.

- Only two Blue Jays have ever won the Cy Young Award: Pat Hentgen and Roger Clemens.

- In 1993, Toronto first baseman John Olerud won the American League batting crown with a batting average of .363, the highest ever by a Blue Jay.

- In 1979, a field-level chair at Exhibition Stadium cost around seven dollars. A seat in the grandstands cost two dollars.

- The first Toronto Blue Jay to hit a grand-slam home run was Hector Torres. He did it on June 27, 1977, against the New York Yankees.

- In 1997, Rogers Clemens knocked off 292 batters via strikeouts.

- The first player signed by Toronto was catcher Phil Roof, obtained from the White Sox before the expansion draft. Roof went to bat five times without a hit before being released by the club.

- As a member of the Blue Jays in 1984, Cliff Johnson collected his 19th career pinch-hit home run to establish a new major league record.

- On September 14, 1987, the Blue Jays played the Baltimore Orioles and set a single-game record by smacking 10 home runs in an 18–3 victory. Leading with the most dingers was Ernie Whitt with three, and Rance Mulliniks and George Bell had two each. The other homers were hit by Fred McGriff, Rob Ducey and Lloyd Moseby.

Chapter Four

Ontario, Basketball's Native Land

The Birthplace of the Creator

Although many websites and books try to claim that James Naismith was an American, he was, in fact, born right here in glorious Ontario in 1961, in the small town of Almonte in the eastern part of the province. Most Canadians know, mainly thanks to the Canadian Heritage Minutes commercials, that Naismith was a proud Canadian. Raised by Scottish immigrant parents, Naismith was no stranger to hard work, but when he had time, he was always involved in team sports and athletics. It was these childhood interests that he returned to later in life when creating a new game he called "basketball."

Seeking new opportunity in the United States, Naismith was working as a physical education teacher at the YMCA in Springfield, Massachusetts, when the track-and-field coach approached him and asked him to come up with some sort of indoor activity that could keep his athletes in shape during the winter but wasn't too rough. Initially,

Naismith had no idea what to tell the coach, but soon he recalled a game he used to play as a child back in rural Ontario called "Duck on a Rock." The game involved two teams trying to knock a rock off a platform by throwing other rocks at it, and although this game may sound nothing like basketball today, the principle of shooting rocks at another team's goal gave Naismith the basic structure for his new game.

In 1891, Naismith devised 13 basic rules, grabbed a soccer ball and two peach baskets and began to work out the details of the game that he would eventually call basketball. Not a bad legacy for a kid from small-town Almonte with memories of Duck on a Rock.

The One and Only

At the inaugural men's basketball event at the 1936 Olympics in Berlin, the Canadians lost the gold medal game to the American squad and took home the silver medal while James Naismith watched from the stands. One wonders who Naismith cheered for. The medal was the only one the Canadian men's basketball team has ever won in Olympic competition.

The Home of Professional Basketball

Just as Americans have tried to claim James Naismith as their own, they also like to think of the National Basketball Association (NBA) as a purely American enterprise, at least before the Toronto

Raptors and the Vancouver Grizzlies came along. However, while the NBA might be based in the United States, the first-ever league game was played on Canadian soil between the Toronto Huskies and the New York Knickerbockers.

In 1946 at Toronto's Maple Leaf Gardens, a crowd of about 7000 fans watched as the Huskies lost the first NBA game by a score of 68–66 to the Knicks. Despite the fact that the first NBA game was played in Canada and hosted by a Canadian franchise, only two Canadian players were on the court that day: Italian-born but Windsor-raised Huskie forward Hank Biasatti and Windsor-born Gino Sovran. Biasatti also holds the distinction of being the only Canadian to have played in two professional sports, in basketball with the Huskies and in baseball with the Philadelphia Athletics.

Although a Canadian had invented the game, basketball was not very popular in Canada at that time. One retired New York player later remarked on playing before a Canadian crowd. "It was interesting playing before Canadians," recalled Sonny Hertzberg. "The fans really didn't understand the game at first. To them, a jump ball was like a faceoff in hockey. But they started to catch on and seemed to like the action."

The Toronto Huskies

Prior to 1946, professional basketball was a series of loosely associated leagues across North America focused on regional competition rather than a full-scale pro league like Major League Baseball. In 1946, the Basketball Association of America (BAA) tried to change all that when a group of arena owners met in New York to figure out how to fill their buildings during the NHL's off-season. The only Canadian invited to the meeting was Frank Selke Sr., who was in charge of operations at Maple Leaf Gardens while Conn Smythe was overseas in the military helping with the post-war cleanup. Selke decided that he would pay the $150,000 franchise fee and establish a basketball team in his city to fill the empty dates at Maple Leaf Gardens. Thus, the Toronto Huskies were born out of a need to fill a building.

After the Huskies lost their first game 68–66 to the Knicks, the 1946 season didn't get any better as they kept losing games, and the fans kept leaving the arena. The team finished the season with a dismal record of 22 wins and 38 losses. With the original $150,000 investment gone, the Huskies closed up shop at the end of their inaugural season, ending professional basketball in Canada until the arrival of the Toronto Raptors and the Vancouver Grizzlies.

On December 8, 2009, the Raptors wore the old Huskies jerseys in a full regular-season game in honour of the city's original basketball franchise. The team put a Huskies banner on their website, and television announcers even referred to the Raptors as the "Huskies" throughout the game.

Birth of the Raptors

Because Toronto already a history of professional basketball, it made the NBA's decision to expand into the Canadian market that much easier. On September 30, 1993, the NBA awarded a group of Toronto businessmen led by Torontonian John Bitove a franchise for a then-record expansion fee of $125 million. The Raptors, along with the Grizzlies, played their first game in 1995 and were the first NBA teams based in Canada.

When talk of a new franchise in Toronto began, many people favoured bringing back the old Toronto Huskies name, but team management quickly realized that it was impossible to create a logo design that wouldn't look just like the Minnesota Timberwolves' logo. Putting the new name to public vote, several names were offered up before the Toronto Raptors was finally settled upon.

In order to bring a little recognition to the club, former NBA legend Isiah Thomas was brought in as the club's inaugural general manager. During the expansion draft, Thomas filled the roster with a selection of young and veteran players. In the subsequent NBA draft lottery, the Raptors selected seventh overall and took Damon Stoudamire, much to the dismay of Raptors fans who wanted Ed O'Bannon of UCLA.

The Raptors kicked off their first year in the league with an opening-game victory over the New Jersey Nets, but they didn't keep up the pace, ending the 1995 season with a record of 21–61. Stoudamire was one of the lone bright spots for the club, winning the rookie of the year award.

Love and Hate

When Vince Carter first joined the Toronto Raptors in 1998, the fans fully embraced the brash, young shooting guard from Daytona Beach, Florida. After several losing seasons since joining the league, Raptors fans loved anyone who looked like he could put numbers up in the win column and help to take the team out of the basement of the league.

With Carter onboard, the Raptors finally had a young flamboyant player that they could build a winning club around, and simply by watching Carter in that first year on the court, you could tell he had the potential to become one of basketball's greats. In his first season, he won the rookie of the year award, and the following year he was selected to the All-Star team. Along with his distant cousin Tracy McGrady, the two power forwards were the centerpieces of the Raptors offense and helped take the Raptors into the playoffs for the first time in 2000. Although they were swept by the New York Knicks in the first round, the Raptors had finally given the fans something to hope for.

Then in 2002, Carter injured his left leg, and the fortunes of the club began to fade without their star player. Fans had already started to question Carter's commitment to the team even though he had signed a six-year, $94 million contract extension with the

Raptors. But then with a continuously injured knee, Carter's star quickly began to fade. He missed the 2002 playoffs and had to sit on the bench and watch as his team was again eliminated in the first round.

By 2004, the Raptors had lost several key players and were looking to rebuilding the club. After several years of struggling with an expansion franchise but little to show for it, Carter expressed his desire to build a winning formula and suggested that the Raptors owner, Maple Leaf Sports and Entertainment president Richard Peddie, should go after some star players he had chosen, but Peddie took the club in a different direction, one that made Carter a very unhappy player.

During the 2004–05 season with the Raptors, it was clear that Carter was not playing up to his potential. He posted a career low of 15.9 points per game and clocked some of the lowest playing time in his career. It was only a few games into the season when the trade rumours began to circulate. It was agreed that something had to be done.

On December 14, 2004, Vince Carter was traded to the New Jersey Nets for Alonzo Mourning, Eric Williams and Aaron Williams and two draft picks. Raptors fans considered Carter a quitter and were happy to see him leave in the end. Their suspicions that he had given up on them were confirmed in a January 2005 interview with reporter John Thompson when asked if he pushed himself hard during games. "In years past, no. I was fortunate to have the talent. You get spoiled when you're able to do a lot of things. You see that you don't have to work at it." After that comment, fans and the franchise were more than happy to turn the page on the Vince Carter era and start anew.

Ontario-born NBA Players

Rick Fox

Toronto-born Rick Fox—along with Steve Nash—is one of the most successful Canadians to play in the NBA, but for Canadians, simply making it into the NBA is an incredible feat, given that only 17 Canadian-born players have ever made it into the NBA.

When Fox was three years old, his family moved to his father's native Bahamas, but Fox retained his Canadian citizenship. After showing promise playing for his high school basketball team in the Bahamas, Fox moved to the U.S. to continue his growth in the sport. He was eventually given a scholarship to the University of North Carolina, where he helped lead his team to the 1991 NCAA Final Four. A highly touted prospect, Fox was drafted 24th overall by the Boston Celtics but played his best years with the Los Angeles Lakers, where he won three consecutive championships from 2000 to 2002.

Although he only spent three years of his life in Canada, Fox played for the national team at the 1994 FIBA Basketball World Championships that were held in Toronto. Despite his help, Canada failed to finish with a medal.

Jamaal Magloire

Born in Toronto, Jamaal Magloire seemed destined to play basketball after shooting up to almost seven feet tall by the time he was 17 years old. However, on top of being freakishly tall when compared to his high school peers, Jamaal was also freakishly talented. After proving himself at the high school basketball level in Toronto, Jamaal won a scholarship to the University of Kentucky where he could play with teammates of equal talent. He was an integral part of the Kentucky Wildcats squad that won the NCAA Division 1 National Championship in 1998.

At the 2000 NBA draft, Jamaal's skills on the court were not overlooked. He was selected 19th overall by the Charlotte Hornets. He has since played for the Milwaukee Bucks, the Portland Trailblazers, the New Jersey Nets, the Dallas Mavericks and currently plays for the Miami Heat. Although the Heat lost the 2011 NBA finals to his old team the Mavericks, Jamaal was signed by Miami for another year because of the veteran skills and leadership he brings to the team. Besides, losing the NBA finals was LeBron's fault, not Jamaal's.

Leo Rautins

Toronto-born Leo Rautins' NBA career was rather short, playing for the Philadelphia 76ers and the Atlanta Hawks for just two years (1983–85). He left the NBA to play basketball in Europe, where he could get more court time. He retired from professional basketball in 1992 and later became a television commentator for the Toronto Raptors. Rautins was named as the coach of the Canadian men's national basketball team in 2005 and retains that position to this day.

Mike Smrek

Born in Welland, Mike Smrek did not stand out during his time in the NBA, but nonetheless he was an integral part of the teams he played for, backing up the starting centres. In total, he played seven years in the NBA. Smrek was drafted by the Chicago Bulls in 1985, traded to the LA Lakers in 1986—where he earned two championship rings in 1987 and 1988—then spent a year with the San Antonio Spurs and finished his NBA career with the Golden State Warriors. Smrek left the Warriors in 1992 to pursue his career in Europe. After retiring from professional basketball in 1997, he moved back to Welland, where he currently teaches at a high school.

Gino Sovran

Born in Windsor in 1924, Sovran played amateur basketball at the Kennedy Collegiate Institute as well as at Assumption College, where he helped the team win the Eastern Canada senior basketball championship in 1946. From there, he joined the newly formed Toronto Huskies. He made his NBA debut on November 22, 1946, against the Boston Celtics and appeared in only six games during that ill-fated season.

Jim Zoet

Born in Uxbridge, Jim Zoet played basketball wherever he could. He played for the Netherlands, England, Argentina, Mexico and the Philippines before finally getting noticed by the NBA. He joined the Detroit Pistons in 1982 but ended up playing only seven games, scoring just two points and quickly ending his professional basketball career.

Ontario Basketball Quick Facts

- The name "Toronto Raptors" was chosen by the public in 1994. Its selection was partially influenced by the 1993 dinosaur film *Jurassic Park* that popularized the velociraptor, which is now the mascot of the team.

- The Toronto Raptors' original team colours were bright red, purple, black and silver.

- Former NBA legend Isiah Thomas was selected as the Raptors' first general manager.

- The Raptors won their first official NBA game in 1995 by a score of 94–79 over the lowly New Jersey Nets. The Raptors ended up finishing the season with a pathetic record of 21 wins and 61 losses.

- Vince Carter was drafted fifth overall by the Golden State Warriors. The Raptors sent Antawn Jamison to the Warriors in return for Carter.

- The Toronto Huskies lasted only one year in the Basketball Association of America, in 1946. The Huskies' leading scorer Mike McCarron scored 649 points in 60 games that season.

Chapter Five

No Longer Fringe Sports

Soccer

Soccer Gold

It seems unimaginable today, given the poor ranking of the Canadian men's national soccer team, but at one point, Canada was the best in the world at the beautiful game. At the 1904 Games in St. Louis, Missouri, a group of players from the Galt Football Club defeated all challengers to bring home Canada's first (and last) Olympic soccer gold.

To put Canada's victory in context, it should be noted that the 1904 Olympics were one of the most sparsely attended games in Olympic history. At the turn of the century, the main mode of transportation was still via land and sea, and most European nations were not willing to travel the great distances needed to get to the United States. So Canada's only competition was whatever teams the U.S. Olympic Committee could scrounge together.

Since soccer was not the most popular sport in North America, the quality of competition was suspect to say the least. Only three teams entered the competition: two from the U.S. and one from Canada. The Galt Football Club had an easy time defeating their American competitors, scoring a total of 11 goals in the tournament while their opponents scored none. Canada was the second country to win a gold medal at the Olympics in soccer (Great Britain was the first).

Toronto FC

Even though the Toronto Football Club was formed in 2006 and has yet to even make it to the championship finals of Major League Soccer (MLS), the team is a hit with fans. Owned by the Toronto-based company Maple Leaf Sports and Entertainment (which also owns the NHL's Maple Leafs, NBA's Raptors and the AHL's Marlies), the club has been well supported by its fans, who have made it one of the most successful franchises off the pitch. The team has been able to pull in a profit since their first season, with regular sold-out games and tons of merchandise sales. Despite its low scoring and an inaugural season record of 6–17–7, the soccer club had firmly established itself with standout players like Danny Dichio.

During their second season in 2008, the club and the city of Toronto took a huge leap forward in the North American soccer world when they hosted the 2008 MLS All-Star Game. The game was a complete success, but the club's season ended in disappointment as they finished in last place in the Eastern Conference.

The next year was another letdown for the fans as the club again failed to make the playoffs, this time by a frustratingly small margin of a single point. To try to turn the tide, Maple Leaf Sports and Entertainment got involved and completely restructured the club by firing their coach and making wholesale changes to the roster. The upheavals seemed to work initially, and Toronto opened up the 2010 season with a series of wins, putting the team near the top of the league by mid-season. However, their streak was interrupted by the long World Cup break, and upon resuming the season, a heavy schedule and untimely injuries brought the club back down to the cellar of the league, missing the playoffs yet again. For the 2011 season, the team's coaching staff was once again overhauled, but as of today, the intended "improvements" don't seem to have changed the club's performance.

Scarborough native Dwayne De Rosario is Toronto FC's all-time leading scorer with 32 career goals (and counting) in 75 appearances. Over 21,800 fans regularly attend Toronto FC games at BMO Field, filling it to capacity. The largest attendance was 22,453 when David Beckham's LA Galaxy rolled into town on April 13, 2011.

Curling

Just a Curling Fact

Ever wonder how that distinctive sound of the curling stone moving down the ice is made? Well, the ice surface in curling is nothing like a hockey rink. Curling ice is deliberately given a rough and bumpy surface so that the stone can travel smoothly over the ice (less contact with the ice surface allows the stone to move faster) and also lets the players "curl" the stone. As the stone moves down the ice, the rough, bumpy surface creates friction between the stone and the ice, giving off that familiar sound. If you listen carefully, it almost sounds as if the rock is saying, "Currrrrrlllllll!" Almost.

Curling Versus the Church

It may be hard to believe, but at one time curling fever gripped the country. The sport became so popular that people were even skipping out on Sunday Mass to attend curling games, often with the shameful intent of betting on the games as well. The problem was that most people in the late 1800s worked six-day weeks and their only day off was Sunday. For them, "And on the seventh day He rested" had become "And on the seventh day he curled."

At first, some churches were willing to ignore that a few members of their flock were disappearing in the wintertime to curl—heck, even a few of the priests could be found on the ice—but when a majority of their congregation began to choose curling over Sunday Mass, some parishes felt they had to act.

In 1888, the Lord's Day Alliance was created under the sponsorship of the Presbyterian Church of Canada in order to fight the increasing secularization of the Sabbath. Their first opportunity to take a stand against curling came in 1903, when a visiting Scottish curling team became embroiled in a controversy during a stopover in Toronto.

The Scottish curlers were well aware of the church's position about curling on the Sabbath, having a reverend on their team and a history in their home country of the church banning curling on Sunday as well. So when the Scots arrived on Sunday, the team planned a visit to Niagara Falls instead of curling. But when Reverend Dr. Milligan of Toronto got wind of their plans, he criticized the Scots from his pulpit for not observing the Sabbath and travelling to Niagara Falls.

The public scolding did nothing to change the plans of the Scottish curlers, so the Lord's Day Alliance changed tactics and began to lobby the federal government to make Sunday a required day of rest and prayer. The lobbyists won out, managing to convince Prime Minister Sir Wilfrid Laurier to introduce the Lord's Day Act into Parliament in 1906. By limiting the operating of non-essential businesses and leisurely pursuits, it was hoped that the new law would leave people with nothing else to do on Sundays but go to church.

The Act went into effect in March 1907, and immediately there was an issue with the new law. Forcing people to go to church was great in theory, but enforcement of such a law was next to impossible. In the more religious parts of Canada, the Lord's Day Act almost policed itself, but in major cities like Toronto, people still insisted on doing what they wanted on Sunday. As time passed and the modern multicultural Canada began to emerge, the Lord's Day Act became more and more inconsequential. Incredibly enough, the Lord's Day Act remained an enforceable law until 1985, when it was removed from Canadian law, though by that time no one even remembered it existed.

Wheelchair Curling

For the able-bodied person, it might seem impossible to conceive of a way that a person in a wheelchair could curl. After all, how could they slide down the ice or even push off from the hack? This was exactly the challenge that drove a few determined curlers to invent a whole new method of curling for those in a wheelchair.

Wheelchair curling got its start in Europe in the 1990s before making its way to North America in the new millennium. In Canada, the first Canadian championship took place in 2004 in London. Although the purpose of the game is still to see who can get the most points by pushing their stones closest to the button, wheelchair curling has a few minor differences. For one, there is no sliding. The wheelchair curler remains firmly in place just short of the hog line and uses a long stick, similar to the one used in shuffleboard, to deliver the stone to the house. Although it's a little more difficult to finesse the picture-perfect shot, the game is as exciting as a regular game.

In 2006, the sport achieved international acceptance when it was added as a medal sport to the Paralympic Games in Torino, Italy. The Ontario curling team had won the right to represent Canada at the Olympics and did their nation proud, bringing home the gold medal with a victory over Great Britain.

Eddie "The Wrench" Werenich

Nicknamed "The Wrench" because he could ratchet up the pressure on and off the ice, Eddie Werenich played an aggressive and highly entertaining style of curling. Born in the small prairie town of Benito, Saskatchewan, Werenich moved to Toronto as a teenager and has always identified himself as being an Ontario curler and a Toronto firefighter.

Werenich's curling career took off in 1972 when he shot as a second for skip Paul Savage. Throughout the 1970s, they curled together and Werenich learned ways to improve his game from Savage. In 1981, Werenich took over as skip, and the pair went on to great successes. At the 1983 Brier, along with Neil Harrison and John Kawaja, Team Ontario beat out a tough Alberta squad to bring the championship back to Ontario for the second year in a row.

For the next 10 years, Werenich remained a top-notch curler while also establishing himself as a royal pain for the Canadian Curlers Association (CCA), whose officials he constantly labelled "freeloading blind mice." He also famously mooned a CCA official, much to the delight of his fan base. Werenich retired from competitive curling in 2000.

Super Howards

Russ Howard is one of the most technically flawless curlers in the game. Besides his great vision for the game, he possesses one of the loudest calls in all of curling.

"Hurry! Hard!" is the notorious call of the wild on the curling sheet, and more than anyone else, Russ Howard has patented the call, making it both a subject to copy for those new to the game and to ridicule for outside observers who find themselves bemused by the Canadian nuances that have come to shape curling today.

Along with his more subdued brother Glenn, the Midland natives have been two of the game's greatest curlers since the late 1980s when they first came on the scene. Although they have split up now that Russ is living and curling out of New Brunswick, some of their best years came with Russ skipping

Team Ontario and Glenn shooting third as they won the national and world championships in 1987 and again in 1993.

Curling Gold!

At the 2006 Winter Olympics in Torino, Russ Howard joined forces with Newfoundland's Brad Gushue to win gold for Canada. At 50 years old, Howard became the oldest athlete to win a gold medal at the Winter Olympics.

A Classic Curling Match

One of the most exciting Brier finals ever was the 1985 Brier between Northern Ontario skip Al Hackner and Alberta skip Pat Ryan.

Like Paul Henderson's goal in 1972, Hackner's shot to win the game has become curling's signature historical moment. In curling circles, it is simply known as "The Shot." The reason it stands out above all others is simple. First, it was Hackner's last chance to snatch victory from the jaws of defeat, and second, it was a shot so improbable that not even magician Criss Angel could have pulled it off.

The final took place on March 10, 1985, at the Moncton Coliseum. Going into the tournament, Pat Ryan's Alberta squad were the odds-on favourites to win the Brier. The Ryan team was known for their heavy-hitting defensive style of game, and if they took an early lead, they would sit on it and take no chances. Remember, these were the days before

Russ Howard invented the "free guard zone," which he designed to usher aggressive and offensive strategies back into the game. But in Pat Ryan's era, he was the master of shutting the game down when he got ahead. So with his team up 5–3 going into the 10th and final end, nobody gave Al Hackner a chance in hell. However, Hackner was never one to give up.

Somehow, after a few shots, Ryan let Hackner get two guards in play, and it was almost Hackner's turn to make the magic shot. With his first stone, Hackner played a textbook split that left him lying one, with another stone on the 12-foot spot. With three stones in the rings (Hackner had an open one on the four-foot line and another on the 12-foot, while Ryan had one in between on the eight-foot), Ryan played a perfect hit-and-roll off Hackner's stone in the four-foot spot. With it, Ryan was now lying two, and both stones were well covered. Hackner seemed finished.

As Hackner stepped into the hack, the crowd of 5000 fell silent. It was clear that his only shot was a razor-thin double takeout. To make it, he needed to slide past his own guard by the thinnest of margins to take out the first Ryan stone. Then his shooter needed to stretch across the house to take out the second Ryan stone. Only then would he lie two and send the game into an extra end. After the match, Hackner recounted his mindset: "I could see about an inch of the rock and I had to hit half an inch. I remember sitting in the hack thinking

I'd made two or three razzle-dazzle shots before in club games, and if I had one more razzle-dazzle in me, let it be now."

Sure enough, he let the stone go and called off the sweepers. As the stone inched past the guard by the scantiest of margins, it was clear that the curling gods were on his side. Hackner nailed the shot, and the arena erupted. With the momentum on his side, Hackner won the game in the extra end.

Inventor

J.S. Russell, a native Scotsman living in Toronto and an avid curler, invented the type of standard curling stones still in use today. After submitting his ideal design to the primary manufacturer of curling stones in Scotland, Russell's stone, with its concave bottom and narrow running surface, was an instant and lasting success.

Ontario Curling Quick Facts

- By around the 1900s, curling clubs in Canada had almost all moved indoors to play their matches as ice-surfacing techniques got better and better and artificial ice became more prevalent.
- In 1927, the Canadian men's Brier curling tournament was born. Named the MacDonald Brier because of sponsor MacDonald Tobacco, it was the first national curling championship in Canada. Eight teams took part that inaugural year at the Granite Club in Toronto in a game

that lasted 14 ends. "Brier" is also a brand of tobacco sold by the competition's sponsor.

- In 1948, the Brier was broadcast live on CBC Radio, helping make the event even more of a curling touchstone since its inception 21 years earlier.

- Up until around the 1950s, curlers in Québec and Ottawa refused to stop playing with the old ironstone stones in favour of the new granite because of tradition and the false belief that they would last longer. The use of ironstone caused a problem when organizing tournaments against other granite-using clubs. This helped to spur a change in the official curling rules, stating that only granite stone be used.

- In 1963, the synthetic curling broom was invented.

- Curling is not normally thought of as a dangerous sport, but the fury of Mother Nature came down on a few curlers in 1974 when a nice day in the hack suddenly turned deadly. A tornado blew through Windsor, peeling the roof off a curling club while curlers were on the ice. Nine people were killed and many more injured.

- In 1998, after years of trying, curling was finally added to the Olympics in Nagano. Canada's Sandra Schmirler won the women's gold while Switzerland took home the men's gold.

- In 2002, the movie *Men With Brooms* debuted in theatres and grossed $1,040,000, proving that the passion for curling is alive and well in Canada.

- Teams from Ontario have won the Brier 13 times as of 2010.

Chapter Six

Ontario Olympians

The Legend of Tom Longboat

Born on the Six Nations Reserve near Brantford in 1887, Tom Longboat grew up in abject poverty. Like most young men from reserves at that time, Longboat was forced to attend Church-run schools where he was not allowed to speak his native language or practice any of his customs. Never one to sit still and listen to authority, Longboat left the school to return to the family farm. After a hard week's labour in the fields, Longboat found solace in long-distance running. He felt free when it was just him against the wind. Running was his escape, and the more he ran, the faster and farther he could go.

Longboat had never thought of entering a race until he met 1901 Boston Marathon–runner Bill Davis. He met the famous Mohawk runner when he was passing through a small town and happened upon a race during the town's summer fair, where Bill Davis was in attendance. Davis took Longboat under his wing and gave the young runner enough confidence to enter into his first race. In the spring of 1905, barely 18 years old, Longboat entered the annual Victoria Day five-mile race in Caledonia. However, Longboat had never trained to run a proper race, and when the gun sounded, he took off in a sprint and quickly became exhausted. He ended up losing the race and afterward vowed to follow a proper training regimen. The hard work paid off, and the following year, Longboat returned to win the Caledonia race.

Ready for a bigger challenge, Longboat entered the 1906 Around the Bay Road Race in Hamilton. Past winners of the race included the first Canadian winner of the Boston Marathon, John Caffery, not to mention William Sherring, who would win a gold medal in the marathon at the 1906 Olympics in Athens, Greece, a few months later. At 30.5 kilometres, the Around the Bay run tested Longboat to his very limits. Longboat, though, proved he could take on any challenge and finished the race in a time of 1:49.25.

Racing in local Canadian events was a nice accomplishment, but Longboat wanted to conquer the running world, and his first major challenge was the Boston Marathon. There are marathon races held all over the world, but the Boston Marathon was (and still is) the most prestigious, drawing in all the best runners. Winning the Boston Marathon is equivalent to winning the Stanley Cup.

At that time, marathon running was extremely popular, and Longboat's exploits in previous races had earned him a small level of fame in American newspapers, but after he entered into the 1907 Boston Marathon, he became an instant star. To the public, Longboat held a certain mystique because he was Mohawk, and the sportswriters loved to come up with all sorts of names for him, such as "The Onondaga Wonder," "The Caledonia Cyclone" or the slightly more awkward, "Streak of Bronze." Longboat was up against some tough competition, but he managed to glide his way across the finish line in 2:24.25, a full five minutes faster than the previous record held by John Caffery.

With such ease on the racetrack, Longboat was the favourite to win the gold medal in the marathon at the 1908 Olympics in London. On the day of the race, July 24, 58 runners from around the globe gathered on the front lawn of Windsor Castle before members of the Royal Family. The weather was not a typical London summer—rain the previous day had combined with an extreme heat wave, turning the air thick and humid and making breathing very difficult. Longboat started out the race well and at his normal pace; however, by the halfway mark, spectators began to notice that something was wrong. Several of the runners had dropped out, and Longboat had slowed considerably and his breathing was getting heavy. At the 20-mile mark, he was barely holding onto second place when he entered into a clearing that was open to the heat and blaring sun, and he suddenly collapsed from heat exhaustion. Longboat was incredibly disappointed by the dramatic end to his Olympic hopes.

Upon his return to North America, Longboat turned pro and travelled to any town that would pay enough to see him run. With the outbreak of World War I, he enlisted into the army as a dispatch runner serving in France. Upon return from the war, he retired from professional running, no longer the same young man who used to dazzle crowds with his endurance and style. He settled in Toronto where he worked until 1944. Retiring to the Six Nations Reserve, he died of pneumonia in 1949.

Boston Glory

The first runner to win two consecutive Boston Marathons was Hamilton-native John Caffery, who took the top spot in 1900 and 1901. The *Boston Globe* described his second race by saying:

> *The dapper little Canadian cut a slice off the record last year, but hewed a big block off yesterday and set a mark that will probably stand for years unless he returns and makes it three straight.*
>
> *He was never worse than second, and then always within reach of his "towney," Hughson, who cut a killing pace for half the 25-mile course.*
>
> *When Caffrey once took the lead, he ran a steady, well-judged race, never showed the flag of distress and was as cheerful at the finish as though he had only done a practice spin.*

Marathon Man William Sherring

When you picture some of the best marathon runners in the world, the image of Billy Sherring is surely the last person to enter your mind. This 110-pound, sliver of a man stood out in a crowd, especially when placed up against some of the best long-distance runners in the world. But despite his small stature, Canada's Billy Sherring earned his share of respect on the track.

Working as a brakeman for the Grand Trunk Railway in the Hamilton area, Sherring spent his every spare moment jogging around the city. Running was his passion, and he began his competitive career by winning several local races, including the famous Around the Bay Road Race (which was renamed the Billy Sherring Memorial Road Race after his death in 1964). Winning all those races by such decisive margins got Sherring noticed by the Canadian Olympic officials, and in 1906, he was chosen to represent Canada at the Olympics in Athens, Greece. The only problem was that Sherring could not afford to pay for the entire trip to Athens on his own.

In the early 1900s, athletes did not have access to the same resources and funding that most athletes enjoy today and were often left to their own devices if they wanted to contend on the world stage. The Hamilton community tried to rally some cash for Sherring by holding several fundraising events, but their well-intentioned efforts only managed to raise $90, clearly not enough to get him all the way to Greece. Being of Irish descent, Sherring felt that he could count on his God-given luck to get him overseas, so with the $90 that the community had raised, he bet on a horse named Cicely and won. Sherring arrived in Greece seven weeks before the Olympic Games and promptly found a job at the Athens rail station in order to finance his rest of his trip.

On the day of the race, May 1, 1906, the temperature in Athens had climbed to a blistering 37°C in the Mediterranean sun. At the start of the 42-kilometre race, Sherring weighed in at 112 pounds, and by the end of the race, he weighed just 98 pounds, giving a good indication as to the gruelling conditions of the Olympic marathon that day.

From the outset of the race, Sherring led the pack, but by the 29th kilometre, Sherring shared the lead with American runner Billy Frank. For several kilometres, the two runners travelled along enjoying each other's company, but as soon as Sherring felt it was time to break out on his own, he said to his American friend, "Well, goodbye Billy!" and he was off.

When Sherring entered the Olympic stadium, he was met with a wave of applause from the 80,000 spectators gathered to watch the final moments of the race. For his final victory lap around the track, he was accompanied by Prince George of Greece, who ran the entire length of the track while emphatically applauding Sherring's triumph.

A picture taken at the time shows an exhausted but exuberant Sherring near the end of the race, wearing a T-shirt with a large shamrock print for good luck standing next to a very regal Prince George in military-style dress, galloping alongside politely clapping.

For his efforts, Sherring received a golden statue of the Greek goddess Athena and a live lamb. But not all were happy with Sherring's victory. In an extract from the magazine *Spalding Athletic Library*, one writer openly lamented the Canadian's victory: "A Greek did not win the marathon race, and for the good it would have done sport, it is too bad that a runner of that nationality did not carry off the honours. To be sure, we all give credit to W.J. Sherring of Canada."

Despite the tongue-and-cheek praise from a few writers, Sherring returned to his hometown as a conquering hero. The Hamilton city council, who before couldn't find a dime in their coffers to send Sherring to Greece, suddenly came up with $5000 to hand over as a reward, and the city of Toronto added another $500 to Sherring's earnings.

Sherring gave up his competitive running career after his 1906 victory in the marathon and took a desk job as a custom's officer with the city of Hamilton. The runner no one thought could win took his last steps at age 86 and passed away in 1964.

The First Marathon

The Olympic course in Athens that Sherring ran was the same legendary course that was once traversed by the Greek soldier and hero Pheidippides, who ran from the city of Marathon to Athens to deliver the victorious message that the Greeks had defeated the Persian army at the Battle of Marathon in 490 BC. As the story goes, Pheidippides ran the distance between the two cities—about 42 kilometres—without stopping, then burst into the Athenian senate and proclaimed, "We have won!" before he fell to floor and died from exhaustion. Supposedly, this story inspired the creation of a 42-kilometre race called a "marathon."

Walk-race Fight

Donald Linden was Canada's premiere race walker of his time. At the 1906 Olympics in Athens, Greece, the native Torontonian won the silver medal in the 1500-metre walk, losing out on the gold medal to American George Bonhag. The American had already competed in Athens in the 1500-metre race but had been kept off the podium. Looking for another way to earn his gold medal, Bonhag had turned to race walking. He had never competed in a walking race in his life, let alone have any knowledge of the sport, but he figured it would be easy enough.

Before the start of competition, Bonhag approached Linden for some advice on how to compete. Linden was unsure of Bonhag's motives.

"So half-jocularly and half-seriously, I told him what shoes to wear, how to stride, what the rules were, and I really encouraged him to enter," said Linden in an interview with historian Henry Roxborough. To Linden's surprise, on race day he looked across the line of competitors and saw Bonhag on the other end.

But there was one problem with Bonhag's performance in the race. Throughout the entire 1500-metre track, Linden noticed that rather than executing the proper footwork of a race walk, Bonhag half-skipped and half-ran the whole way. At the end of the event, Bonhag skipped across the line in first place with Linden a few metres behind him in second place. Linden wasn't alone in his assessment of Bonhag's abhorrent technique—two of the four judges disqualified Bonhag for improper footwork and took his gold medal away. But rather than letting that be the end of the story, Linden did something he would later come to regret.

Wanting to show the world that Bonhag had indeed cheated and that he was the better race walker, Linden challenged Bonhag to a race between the two of them to decide the real gold medal winner. The officials agreed, and the race was scheduled for the next day at 9:30 AM sharp. Linden was on the track early, as usual, and so was the Crown Prince of Greece, both waiting for the arrival of Bonhag so the race could begin. But Bonhag never appeared, nor did he ever give any explanation for his absence. Then, for some strange reason, the results of the 1500-metre walk were entered into the record books, and Bonhag retained his gold medal while Linden was forced to swallow his pride and accept second best.

"I would have been an easy world's champion," said Linden. "But I surely talked myself out of it."

The Rise and Fall of Ben Johnson

Although he was born on the island nation of Jamaica, Benjamin Sinclair Johnson immigrated to Canada in 1976, where he took up residence in Scarborough. A naturally gifted athlete, Johnson's talents caught the eye of coach Charlie Francis, who convinced the young undisciplined athlete to join the Optimist Track and Field Club. Francis was a former Canadian sprint champion in the early 1970s and was part of the Canadian team at the 1972 Olympics in Munich, Germany, though he did not medal.

Under the tutelage of Francis, Johnson quickly found success on the track. At the 1982 Commonwealth Games in Brisbane, Australia, Johnson won two silver medals in the 4x100-metre relay and the 100-metre sprint. His international coming-out party was at the 1984 Olympics in Los Angeles, where he made it to the sprint finals against the great American sprinter Carl Lewis. In an obvious attempt to rattle the American on his home turf, Johnson purposely false-started. However, the gamesmanship did little to help Johnson beat Lewis, but he did manage to take home a bronze medal in the event. He also won another bronze medal in the 4x100-metre relay.

From 1985 to 1988, Johnson brought his speed to a whole new level and was well rewarded for his efforts. After losing seven straight races to Carl Lewis, Johnson finally defeated the American. At the 1986 Goodwill Games, he broke the 10-second barrier for the first time in competition and broke the 60-metre indoor sprint record with a time of 6.50 seconds. At the 1986 Commonwealth Games, Johnson continued his domination of the sprinting world by winning the gold in the 100 metre, the gold in the 4x100 metre and a bronze in the 200 metre. For all his incredible accomplishments up to that time, Johnson was invested as a member of the Order of Canada in 1987, proclaiming him as the "world record holder for the indoor 60-metre run," and "this Ontarian has proved himself to be the world's fastest human being and has broken Canadian, Commonwealth and World Cup 100-metre records."

Then came the event where Johnson truly established himself as the number one runner in the world, finally dethroning his long-time rival Carl Lewis. At the 1987 World Championships in Rome, Johnson not only beat Lewis in the 100-metre sprint final, but he also set a new world record of 9.83 seconds. The record made Ben Johnson a household name around the world, and soon he was making a million dollars every two months simply by endorsing products. That same year, he was named the winner of the Lou Marsh Trophy as Canada's top athlete, the Lionel Conacher Award as Canada's male athlete of the year and was named the *Associated Press* Athlete of the Year for 1987.

Carl Lewis, however, was not happy about the sudden change in command and publicly lashed out. While never saying Johnson's name, Lewis told the BBC, "There are gold medalists at this meet who are on drugs, that race (Rome) will be looked at for many years, for more reasons than one." Johnson was furious at the accusation and resolved to put Lewis in his place at the 1988 Olympics, setting up a dramatic final. On September 24, 1988, Johnson beat Lewis in the 100-metre final and at the same time lowered his record time to 9.79 seconds. It was an incredible moment for all of Canada, but the euphoria did not last.

Just a few days after the incredible record-breaking win, it was revealed that Johnson had tested positive for steroids. Johnson was disqualified and stripped of his gold medal, and Carl Lewis, who came in second, was given the gold instead. In Canada, Johnson went from being a national hero to a stain on Canada's reputation. Suspended from competition for three years, Johnson tried to make a comeback in 1991 at the Hamilton Indoor Games, but just two years later, he again tested positive for excessive amounts of testosterone and was subsequently banned for life by the International Amateur Athletics Federation (IAAF).

In 1999, a Canadian adjudicator ruled that there were procedural errors in the IAAF's judgement against Johnson, and he was allowed to appeal. This meant that while Johnson was not allowed to compete internationally, he could race on Canadian soil. The only problem was that, given his stigma, no one wanted to race against Johnson. Undeterred by the lack of support, Johnson decided to run anyway at a track meet in Kitchener, but he was forced to run alone against the clock. Then, later that same year, Johnson again tested positive for drugs.

Unable to find a friend in North America, Johnson was hired by Libyan leader Moammar al-Gadhafi to act as a soccer coach for his son, Al-Saadi al-Gadhafi, who wanted make it into the Italian soccer league. Al-Saadi did eventually make it onto an Italian soccer team, but he too was kicked off when he tested positive for illegal substances.

Since 1999, life has had its up and downs for Johnson. In 2006, he was hired as a spokesperson for Cheetah Power Surge energy drink. In the ad, Johnson is mock interviewed and is asked, "Ben, when you run, do you Cheetah?" to which Johnson responds, "I Cheetah all the time." He currently lives in Markham and in 2010 he released an autobiography entitled *Seoul to Soul*. In the self-published book, he writes about his childhood in Jamaica and his life in Canada. He also, for some strange reason, suggests that he was an Egyptian pharaoh in a previous life.

You're Ours, Bailey

Although he was born in Manchester, Jamaica, Donovan Bailey was raised in his adopted home of Oakville. Basketball was Bailey's first love, and he only began competing in the 100-metre sprint part time in 1991 at age 24 and fully embraced the sport in 1994.

Just one year after taking up sprint full time, he travelled to Gothenburg, Sweden, to compete in his first major international competition and, in less than 10 seconds, announced that he had arrived on the scene as someone to watch by winning the 100-metre sprint and the 4x100-metre relay gold medals. The victories were a foreshadowing of things soon to come.

At the Summer Olympics, the 100-metre sprint is the marquee event in track and field, in part because of the mystique of crowning the world's fastest runner. Canadians remembered all too well the feelings of jubilation and disappointment associated with Ben Johnson, and although sports fans desperately wanted to put the incident behind them, they could only do so with another gold medal. Enter Canada's number one hope, Donovan Bailey.

The anticipation in Atlanta's Olympic Stadium at the 1996 Olympics was palpable as the athletes took their positions on the 100-metre sprint starting line—and it only mounted when defending British Olympic-champion Linford Christie double-faulted and was disqualified from the competition. Finally, at the third sound of the gun, the race got off to a clean start. Bailey had never been fast coming out of the blocks, and in the first 25 metres, it looked like he was falling behind the pack. But the moment Bailey hit his stride, there was no stopping him. He sped past all his competitors like a Ferrari passing a bunch of Volkswagen Beetles and crossed the finish line a full stride ahead of his closest competitor. Not only had he won Canada the gold medal, but he had also broken the world record of 9.93 seconds set by American Calvin Smith in 1983 with a time of 9.84 seconds. The embarrassing memories of the Ben Johnson affair were wiped from the collective consciousness of Canadians in just under 10 seconds.

Oh Canada?

For the longest time, it was thought that Canada's first medal at the Summer Olympics was won in 1904 by hammer-thrower Étienne Desmarteau from Montréal. In actuality, the first medal winner for Canada came in 1900 when George Orton of Strathroy won the gold medal in the 2500-metre steeplechase at the Olympics in Paris, France, as well as a bronze medal in the 400-metre hurdles.

What led to the mix-up was that Orton was attending college in the United States before the Olympics, and when it came time to go to the Olympics, the Canadian government would not finance his trip overseas. Not wanting to miss the opportunity of a lifetime, Orton took a plane with some of his American athlete friends, and when he won the medals, it was assumed by all that he had been representing the United States. However, it was later discovered that Orton did not have American citizenship and therefore had won the medals as a Canadian citizen.

Cornwall High Jumper

Competing at the 1932 Summer Olympics in Los Angeles, Duncan McNaughton of Cornwall accomplished something no other Canadian has ever done in the history of the Olympics—he won his country's first and only men's gold medal in the high jump. But things could have turned out very differently for the young athlete. Competing at the 1930 British Empire Games, he was disqualified for diving headfirst over the high bar, which was an illegal technique. His disqualification meant that he could not compete for Canada at the 1932 Games, but luckily for McNaughton, officials reversed their decision and he went on to Los Angeles to win the gold medal with a jump of 1.97 metres.

Silken Heart

Silken Laumann's story is one of chance, tragedy, pain and ultimate redemption—the quintessential Olympic moment. After the 1992 Summer Olympics in Barcelona, this Mississauga native became a heroine to many Canadians and an example of an athlete's determination and will to compete even in the face of insurmountable odds.

By the time the 1992 Summer Olympics came around, Silken Laumann could already call herself an Olympic champion, having won a bronze medal in the double sculls rowing event at the 1984 Los Angeles Olympics with her sister Daniele. In between the Los Angeles and Barcelona Olympics, Silken added to her growing list of medals at various tournaments, winning a silver medal in the single sculls at the 1990 world championships and a gold medal at the same event a year later. In the 1992 Olympics, Silken was favoured to finish at the top of the pack and was looking strong and smooth on the water in her training.

With just under two months before the start of the Olympics, Silken was competing in a race in Essen, Germany. As she was warming up for her heat, the boat of the German men's coxless pair Colin von Ettinghausen and Peter Hoeltzenbein suddenly crashed directly into her boat. In a flash, she saw her Olympic dreams taken away.

Later, Silken recalled that fateful moment, "During my warm-up, this German boat came out of nowhere. It crashed right into my right leg, severing all the muscles, tendons, and ligaments from midway up my right shin all the way to the ankle."

Initial reports from the doctors were that she would never row again, let alone be able to walk normally. It was the worst time in her athletic career. After a little rest and rehabilitation, however, her injuries began to heal faster and she was stronger than originally anticipated. Silken held onto that ray of hope—that she might be able to make it back to the Olympics—but her doctors told her to be realistic. She still had a large, open wound on her leg, and getting into any kind of shape to compete in the Olympics was next to impossible. But that slight chance was all that Silken needed to try even harder to prepare herself in time for the Olympics. For her, the pain was just beginning.

To be completely ready for competition, Silken had to undergo intensive rehabilitation and training that pushed her physical and emotional tipping point almost every day. But throughout the tears and moments of self-doubt, Silken envisioned her Olympic goal, and to her, it wasn't good enough just to compete—she wanted to win.

The weeks of pain and sore muscles paid off when, just five weeks after her leg was mangled, she announced to the world that she would be competing in Barcelona. The global media was impressed that she had returned to competitive form, but anyone who has ever covered athletics knows, it's extremely difficult to come back to winning form after sustaining such a traumatic injury. At best, sports pundits were expecting Laumann to make it out of the preliminary rounds in the single sculls. But Laumann not only made it out of the prelim's, she also powered her way into position as one of the six finalists.

Off the line in the final race, Laumann looked liked she was struggling to keep up with the leaders, but she hung in at a steady fourth place behind the American Anne Marden. Television viewers remember the camera focusing in on Laumann's boat as the physical and emotional strain was etched into every muscle on her face. With about 1000 metres to go, Laumann's exhaustion was clearly visible with every stroke she took. This was an athlete giving her entire being into this one single moment—the essence of sport was contained in Laumann's sheer determination. She found a hidden reserve of energy deep within herself and pushed herself to the limit, edging Marden out at the finish line. Silken Laumann had achieved redemption. Sure, it wasn't gold or even silver, but it was bronze, and to Silken, the medal was priceless.

In the days that followed her dramatic come-from-behind story, Laumann was named Canadian Athlete of the Year and was selected to carry the Canadian flag at the closing ceremonies. She added to her Olympic medal collection again at the 1996 Olympics in Atlanta, where she improved on her previous performance by taking home the silver medal in the single sculls, losing the final race to Belarusian Yekaterina Khodotovich. Silken Laumann retired from competitive rowing after the Atlanta games, going down as one of the greatest Canadian athletes in Olympic history.

Adam van Koeverden

Adam van Koeverden, an Oakville native, first burst out onto the kayaking scene in 1999 when he won a bronze medal in the K-1 1000-metre event at the World Junior championships in Croatia. He later made waves in 2003, claiming a silver medal in same event at the World Championship in Gainesville, Florida. Going into the 2004 Olympics in Athens, van Koeverden was still a relative unknown in Canada, but after taking the gold medal in the K-1 500 metre and a bronze in the 1000 metre, he was suddenly the talk of the Canadian sporting world. His celebrity in Canada was elevated even higher when he was named Canada's flag bearer during the closing ceremonies of the Games and was later awarded the 2004 Lou Marsh Trophy as Canadian Athlete of the Year.

All of the added attention put tremendous pressure on van Koeverden to repeat his previous performance at the 2008 Olympics in Beijing. At the World Cup competition in Poznan, Poland, just before the Olympics, he set a new world record in the K-1 500-metre race, which certainly spoke to how he could handle the pressure. With such grace under fire, van Koeverden was the natural choice to represent Canada as the Canadian flag bearer for the opening ceremonies in Beijing.

The Beijing Olympics, however, did not turn out as he had hoped. Although he did bring home a silver medal in the K-1 500-metre event, he stumbled in the 1000-metre race and failed to make the podium. Still only in his 20s while at Beijing, it is assured that van Koeverden will return to the Olympics in 2012 with his eyes on the podium.

In celebration of his successes on the water, the mayor of Oakville, Rob Burton, decided to name a street in honour of van Koeverden. Adam van Koeverden Street is located near the Oakville Burloak Canoe Club.

Triumph and Tragedy of Victor Davis

Born in Guelph, Victor Davis learned to swim in the pristine Canadian lakes that surrounded his childhood home. All the practice paid off, and when Davis started competing against other swimmers his age, he quickly discovered that he was much faster. The goal of any amateur competitive swimmer is to make it to the Olympics, and as Canada's most promising medal hope in the sport in years, Davis was looking forward to the 1980 Olympics in Moscow. But when the Canadian government decided to boycott the Games because of political differences with the Soviet government, Davis, along with many other Canadian athletes, had to put his dreams on hold. While waiting for the 1984 Olympics to come around, Davis collected a few medals at the 1982 World Championship in Ecuador, where he finished the 200-metre breaststroke with a gold medal and a world record, not to mention winning a silver medal in the 100-metre breaststroke as well.

In the four years since the boycotted 1980 Olympics, Davis had not slowed down, but rather, he had improved. Going in as the favourite in the breaststroke, a huge amount of pressure was on him, but luckily he possessed the type of character that revelled in a high-pressure environment. In his first final, he broke the world record, but it was only good enough for silver, losing out to American swimmer Steve Lundquist by a few tenths of a second. Unfazed, Davis came back to win a gold in the 200-metre breaststroke and established a new world record in the process. He later added a silver medal to his haul in the 4x100-metre medley relay.

During his career, Davis set several world records, won 29 national titles and claimed 16 medals in international competitions. After a long career in amateur sports, Davis retired from swimming in 1989. Shortly afterward, he was struck by a car in a hit-and-run while leaving a bar in suburban Montréal and died a few days later as a result of his injuries. Davis had apparently gotten into an argument in the bar with the driver of the car earlier that evening. He was just 25 years old.

Diving First

Irene MacDonald of Hamilton became Canada's first recipient of an Olympic medal in diving when she took home a bronze in the three-metre springboard event at the 1956 Summer Olympics in Melbourne, Australia.

Little Anne Ottenbrite

Walking into the 1984 Olympics in Los Angeles, Anne Ottenbrite was a complete unknown in the swimming world—even people in her own country knew little about the 18-year-old girl from Bowmanville. But all of that quickly changed.

Like many great Olympic stories, Ottenbrite's path to glory was not paved with gold. Two months before making the trip to Los Angeles, she dislocated her right knee, not while working out but while trying on a pair of high heels. Not about to let a pair of shoes keep her from her dream, Ottenbrite worked hard on her recovery and luckily was healthy enough to make the trip out to the Olympics. She had hoped her bad luck was behind her, but just days before the start of her first race, she suffered whiplash in a car accident. Despite her injuries and unfortunate luck, Ottenbrite shook it all off and was ready to compete in her first event: the 200-metre breaststroke.

Going into the race, she was not favoured to medal, but at the sound of the starting gun, she took a commanding lead on her competition and finished almost a full second ahead of her closest competitor. With the win, Ottenbrite became the first Canadian female to win a gold medal in an Olympic pool. Three days later, she was back in the water, winning the silver in the 100-metre breaststroke and a bronze in the 4x100-metre medley relay. She was almost not able to start the Games, but she definitely finished them in style.

Speed Hurdler

Born in Oshawa in 1980, Perdita Felicien first started competing in track-and-field events at her high school. Before making the leap into hurdles, Felicien began her track career as a sprinter, hoping to model herself after Canadian speedsters Donovan Bailey and Bruny Surin, who had both torn up the track at the 1996 Olympics in Atlanta and brought home several medals, including Bailey's world record–setting gold medal in the 100-metre sprint. Felicien did have some success in the 100 metres, but when she first jumped over to the hurdles, she realized that she had found her calling.

Leaping over the gates seemed to come easy for the young woman, and she proved it when she won the Ontario high school hurdling championship in 1997. In 1998, she continued her reign as Ontario's hurdling champion and added two consecutive Canadian junior hurdling championships to her growing list of accomplishments. With a resumé like hers, it wasn't long before several universities came calling with athletic scholarship offers. She ultimately chose to enroll at the University of Illinois.

In 2000, she moved to the United States and immediately made her presence felt. Competing in the 100-metre hurdles at a university track event, Felicien set the record for the fastest time by a freshman in the National Collegiate Athletics Association (NCAA). She followed that record with a win at the national championships, both indoor and outdoor.

Her university athletics career was so successful that she was named University of Illinois Female Athlete of the Year for three consecutive years and was voted the U.S. Track Coaches Association National Female Outdoor Athlete of the Year.

After an incredible start to her career at the university level, Felicien took her talents to the international stage for the first time in 2003, competing in the 100-metre hurdles at the World Track and Field Championships in Paris. There, she beat out some of the world toughest hurdlers, like Jamaica's Brigitte Foster and American Miesha McKelvy, to win her first international gold medal. That race made Canadians take notice of her. She was named the 2003 Canadian Female Athlete of the Year for winning the first-ever individual gold medal by a Canadian in an international track event.

One of the biggest tests of her young career came in 2004 at the IAAF World Indoor Championships in Budapest, Hungary, in a much-anticipated showdown against legendary American Gail Devers. In the end, not only did Felicien beat the three-time hurdles world champion in the 60-metre race, but she also set a new world record time in the process. Racking up win after win in competitions around the world, Felicien and all of Canada had their eyes focused on one spot: the 2004 Olympics in Athens, Greece. On August 24, 2004, Canadians watched as she approached the starting line in the final medal race of the 100-metre sprint.

Felicien burst out of the blocks with her normal force, but something immediately went wrong. Maybe it was the excitement or maybe it was the pressure of an entire nation weighing down on her shoulders, but when Felicien lifted her leg to jump over that first hurdle, she caught the edge with her back leg and fell. Landing awkwardly, she stumbled into the lane of Russian hurdler Irina Shevchenko and knocked her out of the race as well. Unable to continue and in obvious pain, all Felicien could do was watch as Joanna Hayes of the U.S. ran her way to Olympic glory. Only a few minutes after the race, a CBC reporter interviewed Felicien, who looked into the camera and apologized to all Canadians watching.

Being a determined athlete, Felicien did not let one incident deter her from doing what she loved best, and she returned to competitive hurdling, winning a silver in the 100-metre hurdle at the 2007 World Championships in Osaka, Japan. All of Canada hoped that she would be on the line again for the 2008 Olympics in Beijing, but a foot injury kept her from participating. She continues to train and compete and has her eyes firmly fixed on the 2012 Olympics in London.

Zuper Zelinka

London native Jessica Zelinka almost didn't make the trip to the 2008 Summer Olympics in Beijing to compete in the heptathlon after suffering a plantar fascial tear in her right foot. It would have been a complete disaster for the then–26-year-old, having trained most of her life for the Olympics. However, Zelinka was never one to quit, and she trained even harder to get back into form for the start of the Olympics as Canada's only representative in the heptathlon. Despite having an entire country's hopes riding on her shoulders, she managed to keep negative thoughts from breaking through and remained focused on her goals.

On the first day of the gruelling two-day event at the cavernous Beijing National Stadium (the so-called "Bird's Nest" stadium), Zelinka formed up with her competitors on the line for the 100-metre hurdles. The hurdles were never her strongest event, having only achieved a personal best of 13 seconds, and she was up against some fast competitors. On this day, however, from the moment she started running at the sound of the gun, she held a slight edge over the competition. She ended up finishing in second place with a new personal best of 12.97 seconds and 1129 heptathlon points.

The high jump was next on the heptathlon list. Also not her best event, she stumbled a little, only going as high as 1.77 metres, a few centimetres off her personal best. For her efforts, Zelinka gained 941 points to add to her total. The day got worse for her when, in the shot put event, her best throw was over 1.5 metres short of her personal best, giving her a meagre 790 points. The last event of the first day was the 200-metre sprint. A quick runner, Zelinka hoped to put the last two events behind her and end on a high note. And she did just that, finishing the race with a personal best 23.64 seconds, which gave her 1016 points and a total of 3866 for the day.

On day two, Zelinka had to get through the long jump, javelin and the 800-metre race. She started off well in the long jump, earning 887 points with a jump of 6.12 metres. It wasn't her best long jump, but considering that she had to use her left foot to take off because of the still-nagging injury to her right foot, it wasn't an awful result. Javelin gave her another 742 to add to her total.

By the final event, Zelinka was in sixth place overall. Although she did not have any hope of ascending the podium, she was proud of her position given all the adversity she had been through in the past year. In the 800-metre race, she managed to put in a personal best time of 2:07.99, good enough for 995 points and giving her a total of 6490, establishing a new Canadian record. She didn't win the Olympic medal she had always dreamed of, but she achieved her goal. Zelinka has now set her sights on London 2012, where she is hopeful for the podium and maybe even a gold medal.

Canada's Sweetheart

Many years ago, young Canadian girls played with figurines and dolls modelled after her and wore replica figure skates like hers. Even baby girls born at the time were named after her. After dominating the figure skating world throughout her career, Barbara Ann Scott had become Canada's sweetheart.

Born in Ottawa in 1928, Scott won her first figure skating championship at age 11 and, two years later, became the first female skater to land the double Lutz in competition. She was the picture of beauty and grace on-and-off the ice, and she brought an enthusiasm and excitement that lifted the country's spirit after the hardships of World War II. Canada cheered for her when she became the first North American to win the European and World Figure Skating Championships in 1947. Scott further endeared herself to Canadians at the 1948 Winter Olympics in St. Moritz, Switzerland, when she became the first Canadian figure skater to win a gold medal at any Olympic Games.

Throughout the 1940s and '50s, Scott was the darling of the Canadian sports world, and for her athletic contributions, she was inducted into the Canadian Olympic Hall of Fame in 1948, Canada's Sports Hall of Fame in 1955, the Ottawa Sports Hall of Fame in 1966, the Canadian Figure Skating Hall of Fame in 1991 and finally the International Sports Hall of Fame in 1997. She also has a place on Canada's Walk of Fame, is an officer of the Order of Canada and was appointed to the Order of Ontario in 2009.

Death Spiral

At the 1948 Olympics in St. Moritz, Switzerland, Toronto-native Suzanne Morrow and Kitchener's

Wallace Diestelmeyer became the first figure skating pair to perform the fabled "death spiral" in a competition. Their daring move catapulted them to a bronze-medal finish. The death spiral is performed when one partner (usually the man) braces himself with one skate planted firmly on the ice and uses that stance as a pivot while holding his partner's hand and she extends her body, circling around him with only one of her blades touching the ice.

Skate of Her Life

Prior to the 1988 Winter Olympics in Calgary, the figure skating world's attention was completely focused on the top-two women in the sport: German Katarina Witt and American Debi Thomas. Ottawa-native Elizabeth Manley was Canada's highest hope for a medal, but she was not even on the radar to reach the podium. Even her hometown newspaper, the *Ottawa Citizen*, had written her off as inconsistent and having no chance of matching the performances of Witt and Thomas. Manley herself was simply hoping for a top-six finish.

In the first of the three-part figure skating competition, Manley started her program still reeling from the effects of the flu but managed to finish in fourth place by the end of the day. In the short program, Manley landed all her jumps and all the technical requirements, putting her in third place with only one event left to skate.

In her long program, Manley had recovered from the flu and performed each element of her routine with flawless grace. With each successive jump, the crowd at the Calgary Saddledome cheered her on, becoming louder and louder. In her routine, she pulled off five triple jumps, and when she ended her program at centre ice, Manley put her hands to her face in disbelief at the incredible performance she had just given. Her marks in the long program were good enough for the silver medal. She later went on to win a world championship in 1988 and retired from amateur skating shortly thereafter.

Brian Orser

Born in Belleville, Brian Orser is one of Canada's most successful figure skaters. Known as "Mr. Triple Axle" during his career because of the relative ease with which he performed the difficult jump, Orser first broke onto the figure skating scene in 1980, placing sixth at Skate Canada and then winning his first of eight national titles. That same year, he debuted on the international stage, placing sixth at the World Figure Skating Championships.

Always consistent on the ice, Orser steadily improved his performances, and by the time the 1984 Winter Olympics came around, he was good enough to place second behind American Scott Hamilton. When Hamilton retired in 1984, it was thought that Orser would be the next gold medal champion, but then American Brian Boitano came onto the scene and ushered in the age known as the

"Battle of the Brians." The American got the better of the Canadian in competition, beating Orser for the gold medal at the 1987 World Championships and at the 1988 Winter Games in Calgary. However, throughout his career, Orser had not finished off the podium since 1982—quite the accomplishment.

Today, he remains involved in figure skating as a coach of several top skaters from around the world. He was on the sidelines at the Vancouver Olympics in 2010 helping coach South Korean skater Kim Yu-Na to a gold medal performance.

Elvis is Alive!

Named after "The King" himself, Newmarket-born Elvis Stojko was destined to perform. Unlike many boys his age who wanted to play in the NHL, Elvis knew early in his life that he was going to be a figure skater. Hitting the ice at the tender age of four, Elvis progressed so quickly that, just two years later, he had won his first competition trophy. His rise to the upper echelons of the figure skating world was never assured, but anyone who knew the determined young man was sure that one day he would be standing atop an Olympic podium. Elvis' first big introduction to the figure skating world at large came in 1991 at the World Championships in Munich, when he stunned onlookers by landing a quadruple–double jump combination, the first time it had ever been done successfully in competition.

After missing out on the podium in his first shot at the Olympics in 1992, Elvis went into the 1994 Lillehammer Olympics determined to break into the top three. Skating to the soundtrack from the movie *Dragon: The Bruce Lee Story* in a martial arts–inspired routine, he put in one of the best performances of his life, but it still wasn't good enough for gold. He had always been criticized that his routines were not good enough to score high in the artistic points, and in the end, it cost him the gold medal, which went to Russian skater Alexei Urmanov. Despite the snub, Elvis' fans loved what he did on the ice, and they grew in number after he completed one of the most difficult jumps in skating. At the 1997 Grand Prix in Hamilton, Stojko landed a quadruple-triple combination.

A year later, Elvis travelled to the Nagano Olympic Games, heavily favoured to win a gold medal. Unfortunately, it was not to be. Suffering from a nagging groin injury and the flu, Elvis failed to complete his planned quadruple-triple jump in the free skate and appeared crippled with pain after the long program. Despite having the odds stacked against him, Elvis still managed to win the silver medal. Overcome with emotion in a post-Olympics interview, he broke down in tears when he heard the words of support from his fans.

Elvis skated at the 2002 Salt Lake City Olympics but failed to make the podium. It was only a few months later that he announced he was turning professional and would begin touring around the world. Just four years later, though, he retired permanently from figure skating with a final performance in Barrie at the Mariposa Skating Club where he had trained most of his amateur career. He now focuses his talents on coaching the next generation of figure skaters.

Patrick Chan

When Patrick Chan started nurturing his obsession with figure skating in his hometown of Ottawa at the age of five, he always dreamed of one day making it to the Olympics. Little did he realize that his dreams would one day come true.

Chan began to distinguish himself on the national stage at age 13 when he won the Canadian Pre-novice title. He followed that with a win in 2004 at the National Novice Figure Skating Championship, and then in 2005 won the Canadian Junior Championship. This latter victory earned him a spot on the Canadian junior team and an automatic trip to the World Junior Championships. At just 14 years old, Chan became the youngest skater to ever compete at the World Juniors. He placed seventh overall.

The incredible poise Chan showed at the juniors displayed the heart of a true champion and put his name on the world figure skating map. After Elvis Stojko and Brian Orser left the amateur ranks, Canada had been without a medal hopeful for several years, but now figure skating fans across Canada finally had their next great hope.

However, Chan's career took a slight detour in 2006 when his longtime coach Osbourne Colson died of pneumonia and other complications as a result of a car accident. It was a difficult time for the young Canadian skater who had looked upon Colson not only as a coach but also a father figure. After taking some time off, Chan returned to active competition with a renewed purpose.

After a few more junior-level competitions, he found his groove again and, in 2007, moved up to the senior level. That year, Chan competed in his first Canadian Figure Skating Championship, placing seventh. In 2008, he returned to the Canadian Championships and captured the title. At 17 years old, he was the youngest Canadian to win the title. The following year, he successfully defended his title as Canadian champion.

Winning the Canadian championship was great, but Chan wanted to prove himself on the world stage. He travelled to his first World Figure Skating Championship in 2009 as one of the favourites to take home a medal. Chan's dedication to the sport paid off. His well-honed skills and mastery on his blades helped propel him to second place behind American Evan Lysacek.

In 2010, Chan finally achieved his life-long dream of making it to the Olympics, and as an added bonus, the Games were being held before a home crowd in Vancouver. In his short program, he scored a 81.12, good enough for seventh place.

It was a disappointing spot for the hometown favourite, but ever the competitor, Chan returned to form in the long program and put in a personal best score of 160.30 for fifth overall. Although he left the 2010 Winter Olympics without a medal, Chan is still a young man. One wonders what might come next for the Canadian star from Ottawa.

Lennox Lewis Gold

Although born in London, England, when Lennox Lewis was 12, his family packed their bags and moved to Kitchener, where they enrolled him at Cameron Heights Collegiate Institute high school. It was in Canada where he developed the boxing skills that eventually led him to the Olympics.

Coached by Arnie Boehm, Lewis dominated the amateur boxing scene just six years after first putting on a pair of boxing gloves, claiming the 1983 World Amateur Junior Championship. Lewis wanted to follow up his championship with a gold medal at the 1984 Olympics in Los Angeles, but at just 18 years of age, he showed that he wasn't immune to making mistakes, and he finished fifth overall. The experience of fighting for Canada in 1984 and coming home empty-handed left the competitive fighter wanting another shot at redemption.

Lewis trained even harder, and by the time the 1988 Olympics in Seoul Korea came about, he was considered the top contender for the gold in the super heavyweight category. Despite competing with a broken thumb, Lewis fought his way through the competition and won the gold medal for Canada by defeating future heavyweight champion Riddick Bowe in a second-round technical knockout. The victory gave Canada its first gold medal in boxing in over 50 years. Unfortunately for the Canadian sports record books, Lewis soon left his home in Kitchener and returned to England, where he turned pro. He went on to win the world heavyweight boxing title twice and retired in 2004 with a professional record of 41 wins, two losses and one draw. Even though he stopped competing for Canada, his adopted country never forgot his contributions to the sport and inducted him into Canada's Sports Hall of Fame in 2008.

Other 1988 Medalists

Lennox Lewis wasn't the only Canadian athlete to win an Olympic medal in boxing at the 1988 Olympics. Toronto's middleweight Olympian Egerton Marcus defeated challengers from the Philippines, Yugoslavia, West Germany and Pakistan, before losing out in the gold medal match to West German Henry Maske. Canada's Ray Downey completed the medal sweep with a bronze medal in the light middleweight division.

Crazy Golfer

At 46 years old, Richmond-native Georges Lyon became the first Canadian and the last Olympian to win a gold medal in golf (the sport was only featured in the 1900 and 1904 Olympics). Lyon was late to the game, swinging his first club at the age of 37, but he quickly proved to be a natural at the sport. Considered an underdog to the heavily favoured U.S. team at the 1904 Olympics in St. Louis, Missouri, Lyon went on to defeat his 23-year-old American competitor in the final to win the gold medal for Canada. After the medal was placed around his neck at the ceremony, Lyon proceeded to walk around the clubhouse on his hands in celebration.

Triathlon Gold

The gruelling pace, the blazing heat, the freezing water, the burning muscles, every part of your being telling you to stop and rest with each step—this is just a small sampling of the pains that every Olympic triathlete must face in order to have a chance at Olympic glory.

Ever since the triathlon was added as an Olympic sport in 1904, Canadians have never fared very well. Individually, Canada has done okay for itself in swimming, cycling and running events, but with the three events combined, our athletes have never seemed to be able to make it up onto the podium. Our greatest hope came at the 2000 Olympics in Sydney, Australia, in the form of Simon Whitfield.

Ranked 21st overall in the world, Whitfield wasn't given much hope of winning the Olympic event with so many world-class athletes placing well ahead of him before the start of the Sydney Olympics. Whitfield, for one, was just happy to be attending.

"My goal had always been to get to the Olympic Games as a medal contender," he said in the book *Heroes in Our Midst*. "So on September 12, 2000, when I arrived in the athletes' village in Sydney, Australia, I felt I had accomplished my goal."

On race day, Whitfield packed in among 51 other competitors on the edge of Sydney Harbour and stood ready to dive in the chilly waters (which have been known to contain sharks, by the way). When the gun sounded, Whitfield dove in and began his 1.5-kilometre swim. He emerged from the water in 28th place, knowing that he would have to rely on his background in cycling and running to catch up to the leaders. Luckily, the 27 other competitors in front of him were in a tight pack, and by the time he left the cycling transition zone, Whitfield had pulled within 38 seconds of Australian leader Craig Walton.

On the bike, Whitfield quickly worked off the chill from the water under the glaring Australian sun. During the 6.6-kilometre circuit that ran through downtown Sydney, Whitfield made his way through the pack and began to eke out a tiny lead from the rear group. With only a few kilometres to go, he was in ninth place and within striking distance of the top three competitors. If this was going to be his one chance at an Olympic medal, he had to make the most of it. He almost lost that chance when a rider just a few metres ahead of him miscalculated a turn and crashed, taking down a number of riders. Thinking fast, Whitfield slammed on his brakes and came to a stop just in time to avoid adding to the tangle of bodies and bikes.

Although he was lucky to steer clear of the crash, having to stop in the middle of the race put him back in 27th place by the time he reached the running portion of the race, 70 seconds behind the leader. Whitfield was left with just 10 kilometres to make up the time. Things weren't looking good for the Canadian, but as he said himself, "I believed that the winner of the Olympic triathlon would be whoever could put all the preparation together and was relaxed and confident. But ultimately it would come down to who wanted it most."

Strongest on his feet, Whitfield quickly began to gain ground on the leaders, clearly believing that he wanted the gold medal the most. Close to the end of the race, he found himself in fourth place and closing in on the top three. He passed the third-place runner, and then blew by exhausted French runner Olivier Marceau for second place, with first-place runner German Stephan Vuckovic within striking distance.

Vuckovic made an early attempt to distance himself from Whitfield, sprinting toward the finish line that was still 600 metres ahead, but Vuckovic's premature burst used up any reserve power he had, leaving Whitfield a golden opportunity. Finding the energy from somewhere deep inside, Whitfield sprinted down the last few 100 metres, blowing by the fatigued German triathlete. At the finish line of the most challenging race in the Olympics, Whitfield broke the tape to become Canada's first-ever triathlon gold medallist.

At the medal ceremony, as the Canadian national anthem blared over the speakers, Whitfield bowed his head and began to cry. He had realized his dreams and ran the race of his life at the right time.

The Golden Curl: Curt Harnett

Like many young Canadian boys, Thunder Bay–native Curt Harnett's passion was hockey. He lived and breathed the sport, watching the Saturday night broadcasts of *Hockey Night in Canada*, playing street hockey in the summer and hitting the rinks when it was cold enough in the winter. He was a decent hockey player with dreams of one day making it into the NHL. To stay in shape during the summer, Harnett took up cycling, but he quickly realized that the bicycle was his true calling. He abandoned his dreams of making the NHL and took up cycling full time.

Harnett stormed onto the cycling scene as a teenager with his debut at the 1984 Los Angeles Olympics, where he claimed his first medal, a silver, in the 1000-metre time trials. His finish was only three one-hundredths of a second behind the gold medal winner, Germany's Fredy Schmidtke. Harnett followed his first Olympic medal with a gold and a bronze at the Pan American Games in 1987, a silver at the 1990 Auckland Commonwealth Games in the match sprint and a bronze at the 1992 Barcelona

Olympics with a bronze in the match sprint. He participated in his last competitive race at the 1996 Atlanta Olympics and ended up in a close battle for bronze in the match sprint against his friend Gary Niewand of Australia. Harnett won the bronze and enjoyed every moment of his final race.

"As much as I was disappointed that I wasn't going for gold, I was really enjoying myself and living in the moment. It was the final race of my career and it was the best race I ever had in my life. It's time to get a haircut and get a real job."

Harnett cut his trademark long, golden, curly locks and hung up his bicycle. He left the sport as the only Canadian cyclist to win three Olympic medals, and for his accomplishments, he was inducted into the Canadian Olympic Hall of Fame in 2006.

Anne Heggtveit

Not many top-level skiers in Canada come from Ontario—after all, the highest point in the province is the Ishpatina Ridge at just 693 metres, whereas, for comparison, flat Saskatchewan's highest peak, Cypress Hills, measures in at 1468 metres. Surrounding our nation's capital are even smaller "mountains" that, when compared to many European ski resorts, look more like foothills. This is the main reason why Ontario has never really produced any Olympic skiers—that is, until Anne Heggtveit came along.

Born in Ottawa in 1939, Anne Heggtveit's ascension to the crown of Canadian world-class skier was made a little easier because she was raised in a skiing family. Her Norwegian-born father was the 1934 Canadian cross-country skiing champion, and Anne also had two uncles who represented Canada in skiing at the 1932 and 1936 Olympics. Although she was an excellent cross-country skier, Heggtveit craved the excitement and thrill of downhill skiing. Using the Gatineau Hills as her training ground, she set about making the jump from cross-country to alpine.

At the age of 15, Heggtveit competed in her first international event in 1954 at Norway's Holmenkollen ski hill. Competing in the giant slalom event, Heggtveit stunned her older and more seasoned competition by coming in first. No one gave the young girl from the flat capital of Canada any hopes of competing against the European-trained skiers, but when she was done carving up the Norwegian mountains, every competitor surely remembered her name.

After witnessing her incredible results on the slopes, the Canadian ski team added her to the roster for the 1956 Winter Games in Cortina d'Ampezzo, Italy. This time, the 17-year-old rookie looked out of place among the best skiers in the world and finished 22nd in the downhill event. It was a lesson learned for the teenager, who did not let it go to waste.

After injuries removed her from the slopes for much of the late 1950s, she was back in competitive form by 1959 and racing in tournaments across North America and Europe. Her time off from the sport seemed to do her good. She won her first major European competition in St. Moritz, Switzerland, placing first in the slalom event and first in the alpine combined. By the time the 1960 Squaw Valley Winter Olympics rolled around, she was one of the favourites to compete for gold. However, she did not start out well, finishing 12th in the downhill and giant slalom events. She had one shot left at gold in the two-run, total-time slalom event.

Perched on the edge of the mountain, Heggtveit launched herself out of the starting gate with all her might. She dogged the gate with the precision of a brain surgeon and finished the course in 54 seconds flat. Barring a complete disaster in the second run, Heggtveit had all but wrapped up the gold medal. For her second run, she had to decide whether to ski the course conservatively to safeguard her number one spot or to blaze down the hill and guarantee no challengers.

Of course, she chose to attack the course and ended up finishing with a time of 55.6 seconds. Totalling her times, she beat out her closest opponent by a whopping 3.3 seconds. Her slalom win not only established the record for the largest margin of victory in an alpine event but also garnered her the first Canadian gold at the 1960 Olympics.

Wanting to go out on top, Anne Heggtveit retired from competitive skiing after the Olympics.

Ski Queen Nancy Greene

Named Canada's top female athlete of the 20th century by *The Canadian Press* and *The Broadcast News*, alpine skier Nancy Greene has long been our nation's source of pride in the history of competitive skiing, especially since so few Canadians have excelled to such heights.

Born in Ottawa in 1943, Nancy Greene and her family moved to Rossland, British Columbia, when she was three years old. She fell in love with skiing from the moment they arrived in BC and proved to be a natural on the hills around her home. As she grew up, Greene moved quickly through the competitive ranks. By the time she was 24 years old, she had won several junior championships and Canadian national titles, and in 1967, she edged out some very tough European competition to win the overall World Cup. Just one year later, she was at the Winter Olympics in Grenoble, France, where she won the gold medal in the giant slalom and the silver medal in the slalom.

For her efforts on the slopes and in Canadian sports, she was awarded the Bobbie Rosenfeld Award in 1967 and 1968 as the top female athlete in Canada. Despite being at the top of her game, Greene decided to retire shortly after Grenoble. She continued to be active in the ski world, teaching new Canadian Olympic hopefuls until she was named to the Canadian Senate in 2008 by Prime Minister Stephen Harper and brought back to the city where she was born.

Can't Get Enough Duff

Born in Vaughan, Duff Gibson had always loved sports. He competed in wrestling, bobsleigh, speed skating and rowing, but he had never really turned his athletics into a career. He was more than happy living his life in Calgary as an airport firefighter. However, when Gibson was first introduced to the sport of skeleton, everything changed for him.

Although luge is the more recognized of the individual winter track sports, skeleton has been around for a long time. The first skeleton event took place at the Olympics in 1928 in St. Moritz, Switzerland, and again in 1948 in St. Moritz before disappearing until the 2002 Olympics in Salt Lake City as a full medal sport.

Skeleton looks and operates almost exactly like singles luge, but instead of pointing their feet down the track, the skeleton riders put their face forward. A run starts with the athletes running on the ice for a few metres before diving belly-first onto the sled. With their arms and legs all tucked in behind them, the athletes must use only their bodies and the force of gravity to steer the sled down the track.

Canada had never fared well at the Olympics in the bobsleigh or the luge events, but ever since the sport of skeleton was re-introduced, Canadian athletes have been carving out a place in the international spotlight. After a disappointing first foray at the 2002 Olympics, Canadians returned in 2006 to dominate the field, and the first athlete to take home a gold medal was none other than Duff Gibson.

At 39 years old at the time, Gibson was not given much chance of beating a younger field of athletes, but he proved that you can never underestimate experience over youthful power. Gibson hit the track and blazed down at speeds over 100 kilometres per hour, finishing the course in 1:55.09 to win Canada's first-ever gold medal in the event. Gibson just happened to beat young Canadian Jeff Pain, who put in an equally amazing performance to take home the silver medal. On the women's side, Mellisa Hollingsworth won the bronze medal, giving Canada three medals in one event.

Gibson's win at the Olympics allowed him to surpass fellow Canadian Al MacInnis as the oldest gold medallist in Canadian Winter Olympics history, and it also made him the oldest individual to win gold at the time, beating out 35-year-old Magnar Solberg of Norway, who won gold in the 20-kilometre individual biathlon at the 1972 Winter Games. Russ Howard, a Canadian curler, has since taken the title of oldest Olympian after winning gold in the 2006 Olympics.

Hockey at the Olympics

The Toronto Granites

Long before the hockey nations of the world sent a selection of their best players to the Olympics, they would send their best teams. At the first Winter Games in 1924 in Chamonix, France, the Granite Club players from Toronto were sent to represent their country. The Granites had no idea the calibre of teams they would be facing in France, but they were prepared for anything because playing against the tough teams in the South Ontario leagues had given them plenty of stiff competition.

However, the Granites were certainly not ready for the conditions that awaited them in France. Ice hockey as a sport had not yet taken hold abroad, and the Olympic organizers had not prepared the rinks up to the standards that the Canadian players were used to. First off, all the rinks were outdoors, making the ice conditions a slave to the weather. Second, the boards around the rinks were only about 30 centimetres high, and there was the constant worry of causing avalanches because the rinks were situated directly at the base of Mont Blanc, a spot known for frequent whiteouts.

But despite these conditions, the Toronto Granites performed exceptionally well. Looking back, they were likely too seasoned for the level of competition that the international community threw at them— the Canadians dominated the round-robin portion of the tournament, beating Czechoslovakia 30–0,

Sweden 22–0 and Switzerland 33–0. It must have been almost comical to watch the speedy Canadians dance around the hapless European players. The Canadian forwards controlled the games so much that their goaltender Jack Cameron had a tough time remaining interested in the game and was frequently spotted skating over to the crowd to chat up the young women in attendance.

In the semi-final rounds, Canada was up against Great Britain. The Brits were tough opponents, but the Granites still came out with a decisive 19–2 victory. The final game, however, turned out to be more of a challenge. The United States had a much deeper history of playing hockey than the other teams and was able to ice a higher-quality team, but even against a tougher opponent, the Granites defeated the U.S. by a final score of 6–1. It was the second Olympic hockey gold for Canada after having been awarded a hockey gold medal at the 1920 Olympics in Antwerp, Germany.

Toronto Grads

At the 1928 Olympics in St. Moritz, Switzerland, Canada chose the University of Toronto Varsity Grads to represent the country in the hockey tournament. The Grads were one of the most talented amateur teams in Canada, just off a winning season where they took the Allan Cup in 1927, and they just happened to be coached by Conn Smythe, also owner of the Toronto Maple Leafs.

The Grads were used to the pressure of crucial hockey games and had done battle with some of Canada's best teams. Even before the tournament in St. Moritz started, most of the fans in Canada had already begun celebrating the gold medal, especially after Canada's last performance at the Olympics. For this reason, Olympic organizers decided to try a different format for the 1928 hockey tournament. Instead of the regular round-robin format followed by a series of playoffs, the organizers divided the 10 teams that were registered for the event into three separate pools plus the Canadians. After a few preliminary games, the winner of each pool went on to play the Canadians. The organizers wanted to ensure that the Canadians faced only the teams that were good enough to at least put up a respectable challenge.

However, leading up to the start of the Olympics, the Toronto Grads were dealt a blow when Conn Smythe suddenly pulled out as their coach to focus on his increasing involvement with the NHL and the Toronto Maple Leafs. Smythe's departure left the head coaching job to assistant coach W.A. Hewitt and his new assistant coach, a wet-behind-the-ears Harold Ballard, a future owner of the Toronto Maple Leafs.

First out of the gates was Sweden, whom the Canadians promptly sent home with an 11–0 victory. Great Britain did not offer much of a challenge this year either, losing the game by an even larger margin of 14–0. And despite the backing of the home crowd, the final team facing Canada for the gold medal was the Swiss team, but they provided no challenge for the Grads, who won handily by a final of 13–0. The Canadians won the tournament by a combined score of 38–0.

After winning the gold, the Canadian team embarked on a whirlwind tour of Europe, stopping in Vienna, Berlin, Paris and London. Fans by the thousands came out to greet the Canadian Olympic champions and to see how the game of hockey was supposed to be played. After being celebrated all across Europe, the Grads returned home as world champions.

Port Arthur in Hitler's Germany

Under the watchful eye of Adolf Hitler and the National Socialist Party, the twin German towns of Garmisch-Partenkirchen played host to the fourth Winter Olympic Games in 1936. The Olympics are supposed to be about the nations of the world coming together in the spirit of friendship and understanding, but when Germany was awarded the Games, the world had not yet fully grasped the nature of what the country was about to become.

International Olympic Committee (IOC) president Henri de Baillet-Latour experienced a taste of Nazi hospitality when, on his way into the town of Garmisch, he saw a sign that read "Dogs and Jews not Allowed." Baillet-Latour demanded that the sign be taken down at once, but Hitler replied that, as a guest of the host nation, the IOC should accept and understand the host culture. However, when the IOC president threatened to cancel the Olympics, Hitler capitulated and had the sign removed.

Canada's team of choice for these Olympics was the Port Arthur Bear Cats. The Bear Cats had lost the Allan Cup final to the Halifax Wolves, but because many of the Wolves players had turned professional before the Olympics, the Bear Cats were chosen to fill in.

The Bear Cats got through the opening games of the hockey tournament in convincing fashion, beating Poland, Latvia and Austria. Canada's first opponent in the medal rounds was Great Britain, a team that had since been stacked with Canadian expats. During the game, the Brits repelled the Canadian attack, thanks in large part to save after save by British/Canadian goaltender James Foster. He had learned a few things during his years in the Canadian hockey system, and he was absolutely spectacular versus Canada at these Olympics. Because of Foster's acrobatic efforts, the Brits managed to defeat the mighty Canadians by a narrow 2–1 margin.

The Port Arthur Bear Cats brushed off the defeat with their heads still held high, knowing that they would probably get another chance at the Brits later on. The Bear Cats stuck to their game plan and defeated the Czechs and the Americans and were all set to play the Brits for the gold medal, but the game never took place.

Out of the blue, Olympic authorities suddenly changed the tournament format after the second round. The second-round matches now counted in the third-round standings, meaning that Canada's early loss to Great Britain virtually eliminated them from competing for the gold medal. Canadian Olympic official P.J. Mulqueen called it "one of the worst manipulations in sports history."

Great Britain, with just two native British players on the team (the rest were solely Canadians), was handed the gold medal, and the Canadians got the silver medal as a consolation prize. The Port Arthur Bear Cats departed the games with the historical stigma of being the team that ended Canada's four straight gold medal reign in the Olympics. However, members of the Bear Cats had to have felt some consolation as most of the "British" players were mates from towns near where they grew up.

Chapter Seven

Golfing Ontarians

We're Number One!

A 2006 study by the Royal Canadian Golf Association stated that 21.4 percent of Canadians over the age of 12 have played golf more than a few times in their lives, compared with only 18 percent in the United States. Of those Canadians hitting the links, 71 percent are male and 29 percent are female. The study also detailed that Ontario leads the stats with 39 percent of Ontarians having played or still play golf. The Atlantic region had the least amount at 7 percent of the national total.

Mike Weir

One of the greatest individual achievements in the last 25 years of Canadian sports came in 2003, when Sarnia-born Mike Weir won the Masters Golf Tournament. Many Canadians watched their television screens in the final moments of the tournament to see Weir sink a seven-foot putt on the 18th hole to force a playoff with Len Mattiace. A simple tap-in putt on the first playoff hole sealed the deal, making Weir the first Canadian male golfer to ever win a professional major championship.

However, Weir has been far from a one-hit wonder on the course. In his 20-year professional career, he has won eight times on the PGA Tour and has finished in the top 10 in all four major championships at one point in his career. He has over $27 million in career earnings and stands 11th on the all-time money list. In 1999, he became the first Canadian in 45 years to win a PGA tournament on home soil when he won the Air Canada Championship in Surrey, BC. Before a decidedly biased crowd at the 2004 Canadian Open, Weir lost a heart-breaking playoff to Vijay Singh, coming within a hair to bringing home the title for the first time since 1954 when Pat Fletcher won the event in Vancouver.

At first glance, Weir is an unimposing sports hero. He stands just 5-foot-9 and weighs a slight 155 pounds. However, that small-framed man spends hours in the gym developing the muscle he needs to improve his golf game, and he is all business on the golf course, playing with a determined look in his eyes and a quick pace from shot to shot. You don't become the best in the world without working hard.

Mike Weir grew up in Brights Grove, a small community on the shores of Lake Huron, a few kilometres north of Sarnia, where he was born in 1970. Introduced to golf at the age of eight by his father, Weir enjoyed the game but was more passionate about hockey. However, at the age of 10, when the Weir family moved into a new house across the street from the Huron Oaks Golf Club, Weir's athletic passions quickly changed. Every day in the spring and summer, Weir could be found down at the clubhouse, playing when he could and caddying when he had to. In September 1981, Jack Nicklaus played an exhibition game in Brights Grove against Steve Bennett, the Huron Oaks club pro. An 11-year-old Mike Weir followed Nicklaus around the back nine, watching how the living legend carried himself and how he prepared for each shot. Nicklaus took every stroke seriously, and it was that dedication that Weir tried to emulate in his game.

After hours and hours of practice, Mike Weir began competing in junior tournaments. By the time he was 14, he entered into a local junior tournament and ended up shooting a 70, beating golfers as much as five years older than he was. Ever the perfectionist, Weir felt he could do much better and contemplated switching from his natural left hand to a right-handed shot. Unsure of what to do, he sought out the advice of Jack Nicklaus by writing him a brief note: "I want to be a professional golfer. I play left-handed. Do you think I should switch?" A month later, he received a reply: "I have always believed that a left-handed player is better off sticking with his natural swing." Not wanting to disobey Jack Nicklaus, Weir stayed a lefty. With a little hard work, Weir ironed out the kinks in his game and was back on track.

In 1985, Mike Weir's stock in the golf world began to rise. He finished second at the Ontario Junior Golf Championship, won two other tournaments and was in the top 10 in all 15 events he entered that year. In 1986, he added four more tournament wins, playing in a popular junior series called the Junior Tyson Tour, and later in the year, he won the Canadian Juvenile Championship in Edmonton.

After a stellar amateur career, Weir finally made it into the professional ranks in 1997 and joined the big boys on the PGA Tour. However, like most rookies to the tour, Weir struggled his first year out, missing the cut in 14 of the first 26 tournaments he tried out for. By the time he came to the last tournament, he was 126th on the money list rankings. This was significant since only the top 125 money winners got to play on the Tour the following year—players who were ranked lower had to battle it out in qualifying school to earn their return tickets. After the shaky start and paying his dues just to qualify, Weir turned his game around during the 1999 season, with a series of top-20 finishes that put him higher up on the money list. He even finished in second place at the Western Open behind golf's most recent superstar, Tiger Woods.

Over the next three years, Weir accumulated a nice series of top-10 finishes and even a few tournament wins on the Tour. He was now earning millions of dollars per year and finally getting the recognition he had always wanted as one of golf's better players, but he still did not have a major tournament win. To even be considered as one of the best golfers in the world, you needed to have a major tournament such as the British Open or the Masters on your resumé. In 2003, Weir finally accomplished that dream by winning the Masters and getting to join the likes of Jack Nicklaus and Tiger Woods in that exclusive club of green-jacketed golfers.

Since the Masters, Weir has had his ups and downs on the golf course, but his passion for the game remains consistent. Although his last PGA tournament win came in 2007, he has remained in or close to the top 10 in most tournaments and has managed to still bring home a salary in the millions. In 2010, Weir suffered a torn ligament in his right elbow and was forced to pull himself out of the Tour and has since failed to return to form, but if anything, this injury will make him work even harder to get back into the game and compete. It's just something Mike Weir has always done.

Mike Weir Canadian Fact

After winning the 2003 Masters, Weir was allowed to clear the clubhouse refrigerator of beer and take the booze back to his victory party at a rented house full of his Canadian friends. No word on whether the beer was Molson Canadian.

Weir Wines

On top of his passion for sports, Mike Weir loves his wines. It is a family tradition that started with his Italian grandfather, who used to make wine in his basement and sneak a few sips for his curious grandson whenever he came to visit.

Mike Weir moved on in life, enjoying the occasional glass of red and white wine but never gave the subject much thought until 2004, when he hosted the Champions dinner at the Augusta National Golf Club. He had heard of a new growth in the popularity and quality of Niagara-region wines and insisted that all the wines served at the Champions dinner be from his native province. The wines proved a huge success, and thus started Weir's idea of starting his own winery. A year later, in April 2005, he launched the first Mike Weir–brand wine. On his winery website, he writes about how his passion for wine and golf are very similar:

> *Making and creating wine is a passion, just like golf. Wine to me is a journey. You start out trying a few things and the next thing you know, your reading, buying more wines, learning more and eventually collecting. Then one day—you're planting grapes in your front yard! Golf is very much like that too, and I suppose it's why I am so passionate about both. Before you know it, you're buying better clubs, playing nicer courses taking lessons, etc.*

Since opening his Niagara-based winery, Mike Weir has expanded his selection to include a rosé, a sauvignon blanc, a Riesling, a pinot noir, a chardonnay and (this author's personal favourite) a cabernet merlot.

Sandra Post

Ask Canadians who the country's best golfer is and most of them might point to Mike Weir. But what most people forget is that our Canadian women have been playing the game just as long as, and in some cases even better than, the men. Take the case of Sandra Post, an energetic player from Oakville.

Post grew up on a 25-acre fruit farm and was introduced to golf at the age of five after her father took her to an LPGA tournament while on a family vacation in Florida. From that day on, she was hooked on the sport, and by the mid-1960s, she had begun to move up in the women's golf ranks, eventually making the LPGA in 1968. Not one to do things in half measures, Post won a major and then the entire LPGA championship in her first season, something her Canadian male counterparts have never accomplished. She went on to win eight LPGA tournaments and a host of other events all over the world.

In 1979, Post was awarded the Lou Marsh Trophy as Canada's best athlete. When she retired, Post was the seventh leading money winner in LPGA history—a golf resume like this cannot be found among Canadian men.

"My parents always wanted me to be a professional golfer," said Post after retiring. "Some parents want to sent their kids to school; mine wanted me to play golf."

Post is lucky that she listened. Although women's golf still has not earned the respect and attention of the men's tournament, there is no denying the sheer talent that Post displayed throughout her career, truly making her one of Canada's greatest golfers.

Not So Incredible Tournament

Golf is a sport of rules, and without rules, the game would be chaotic. However, on occasion, these rules can be a tad strict. This is exactly what American golfer Andy Bean found out during the 1983 Canadian Open at the Glen Abbey Golf Course in Oakville.

With a few holes remaining, Bean found himself several strokes off the lead but still within striking distance of the leader, who had already finished his tournament. Just four strokes separated first from fifth place. Bean would have to pull off a miracle in the final holes, but anything is possible in golf—a few birdies and he could easily take the Canadian championship.

On the par-four 15th hole, Bean smacked a beautiful drive, setting himself up for a second and third shot that put him within inches of the cup for an easy par. With just two inches of grass between his ball and the cup, Bean figured he had sealed his par, but he got caught up in the excitement of the moment and flipped his club upside-down and tapped the ball in with the handle of his putter. Little did Bean realize that Rule 19 of the official rulebook of golf states, "The ball shall be fairly struck at with the head of the club." It seems silly to punish a player for hitting the ball with a part of the club that clearly does not offer any advantage over hitting it with the head of the club, but the rules are there for a reason, and they had to be enforced.

Bean was given a two-stroke penalty, and he ended up finishing the Canadian Open in fourth place, just two strokes behind co-leaders John Cook and Johnny Miller. Cook later won the Open in a playoff round against Miller. However, it might have been a blessing in disguise for Bean because Cook and Miller went on to play the longest sudden-death playoff in Canadian Open history, needing six holes to decide the eventual winner.

Old Rookie Stan Leonard

Not all sports stories start out the same. While people like Wayne Gretzky and Mike Weir began their athletic careers at an early age and remained focused on their goal of making it to the top of their chosen profession as fast as their talent would take them, some athletes choose a much different route.

In 1955, at the ripe age of 40, Sarnia-native Stan Leonard decided to leave the safety of his job as the head pro golfer at the beautiful Marine Drive Golf Club in Vancouver to head south and give the PGA Tour a real try. It was a difficult choice for the aging golfer, especially going up against golfers nearly half his age, such as Ben Hogan and Sam Snead, but Leonard knew that his experience would help him. However, it was not like he appeared out of nowhere.

Leonard had dominated the Canadian golfing scene for over 20 years, winning 40 national titles, including eight Canadian PGA Championships and notching five second-place finishes. He also captured nine Alberta Opens, five BC Opens, two Saskatchewan Opens, a couple of Canadian Match Play titles and was named the best Canadian pro at eight Canadian Opens.

After making the 1955 American PGA Tour, Leonard finished eighth in his first competition at the San Diego Open. He continued to post good results on the Tour, winning a few tournaments here and there, but the money wasn't as abundant as it is today.

"If you won a 1000 bucks in a week, you had a good week," said Leonard in a 1983 interview. "Of course, things were different. We went by car, maybe a day's drive...Now all tournaments have a central hotel, and everything is laid out for the players. We used to drive around and find a cheap motel. One of the guys would say, 'Hey, there's one down the street for $10, and we'd all go there.'"

Leonard continued earning enough to make a decent living until retiring from professional golf in 1971. He moved to Florida, where he became the director of golf at the Desert Island Golf and Country Club in Palm Springs, a position he held until 1991. In 2005, at the age of 90, this enterprising Canadian golfer died.

Al Balding

This Toronto-born golfer became the first Canadian to win a PGA tournament in the United States in December 1955 when he won the Mayfair Inn Open in Miami, beating out U.S. Stars like Sam Snead and Tommy Bolt. Balding also teamed up with Canadian golfer Georges Knudson in 1968 to win the World Cup Team Championship of Golf.

The Golf Savant

Only two men own their golf swings, Ben Hogan and Moe Norman.

–Tiger Woods

Murray Irwin "Moe" Norman was one of the most colourful personalities in Canadian golf history, and even though few people have ever heard of him, during his time, this Kitchener-born golfer had the best pros in the world singing his praises.

Born in 1929 and growing up during the Depression, his family noticed early on that Moe was not like other children. He exhibited symptoms of social anxiety, spoke rapidly for no reason and would often repeat himself. Some of his family members thought it was because of an accident Moe suffered as a child when he was run over by a car, but it was revealed much later that he suffered from autism. Like most other autistics, Moe showed a remarkable agility with numbers. His card-counting ability made him almost unbeatable at poker, he could remember the exact number of golf courses he had played on and, in many cases, the exact yardage of each hole he'd ever shot.

Norman learned to play golf at the age of 12, when he became a caddie at the Westmount Golf and Country Club in Kitchener and would sometimes sneak onto the course to play a few holes himself. Norman was not a natural golfer, but the sport quickly became his obsession. He spent hours improving his swing, and by the time he was 17, he was shooting in the low 70s. At 19, he won his first tournament. He was becoming a great golfer, but what brought him the most attention were his trick shots. Crowds would gather and watch as Norman would hit the ball off of a series of high tees, including one that was eight inches (20 centimetres) off the ground. Once, he entertained a crowd by bouncing a golf ball on the head of one of his irons 184 times straight without interruption. He made his living travelling across the provinces playing in small amateur tournaments, winning what money he could, and everywhere he went, no one ever forgot the name Moe Norman.

By 1954, now 34 years old, Norman had played his way to the number one ranking amateur in Ontario, but this was only the beginning of the Norman odyssey. In 1955, he won the Canadian amateur title, giving him an automatic spot in the upcoming Masters.

At the Masters, he hit every ball off the tee straight and true, but the presence of the large crowds and TV cameras unnerved him, and as a result, his short game suffered. After the first two rounds, Norman was well behind the top spot. Killing time in between the rounds, he was at the practice range working out the kinks in his game when he was approached by the legendary golfer Sam Snead, who offered him some swing advice to improve his short game. Norman immediately took Snead's words to heart and was determined to master what he had told him. A little practice is good, but Norman could never tell when enough was enough. For the rest of the afternoon and evening, he shot a total of 800 balls trying to perfect his swing. The next day, his hands were so red and raw from all the swings that he could barely hold his clubs and was forced to withdraw from the tournament.

Norman played professional golf through the 1960s, '70s and early '80s before his age finally started catching up with him. As he got older, he made less and less money, and once had to be bailed out financially by his friends. As he slowed down, the highlight of his year was showing up at the practice range during the Canadian Open. He would chat with the pros and teach them a few things he knew about golf, Norman-style. Inevitably, he always drew a crowd, and Mike Weir, Tom Watson, Fred Couples, Nick Faldo and the other top professionals would watch in awe as Norman hit ball after ball, straight out into the middle of the fairway. Just before the 2004 Canadian Open, Moe Norman passed away from heart failure. His smiling face can still be seen at the Canadian Golf Hall of Fame, where he was inducted in 1995.

Poetry by Moe Norman
(recited in an ESPN interview in 2000)

I have a little robot that goes around with me.
I tell it what I'm thinking.
I tell it what I see.
I tell my little robot all my hopes and fears.
It listens and remembers everything it hears.
At first my little robot followed my command.
But after years of training it's gotten out of hand.
It doesn't care what's right or wrong
Or what is false or true.
But no matter what I try
Now it tells me what to do.

Chapter Eight

A Wide Variety of Pastimes

Tug-of-War Champions

When most people think of tug-of-war, they think of picnic fun and schoolyard games, not an international sport, but at one time, tug-of-war was a serious athletic pursuit that made it into the Olympics. From 1900 to 1920, tug-of-war was held as a full medal sport in the Olympics.

Tug-of-war was one of Canada's most popular sports in the late 1800s. Our most glorious moment came at the 1888 North American Tug-of-War Championships in Buffalo, New York. Representing Canada at the games were five farmers from the small town of Zorra.

The Canadians were virtual unknowns at the tug-of-war tournament, so no one really paid them much mind, but after years spent on a farm, the five men were tough enough to compete with anyone. Before a crowd of 10,000 screaming fans, the farmers from Zorra yanked every competitor from the safety of their zone and took the championship back to the farm with them.

Old but Strong

In 1971, the Royal York Hotel in downtown Toronto played host to a boxing fight between Clyde Gray and Humberto Trotman. Refereeing that night was former 1940s welterweight fighter Sammy Luftspring, known for his strict but fair officiating. Through most of the fight, Trotman gave Luftspring a tough time, refusing to follow his orders and constantly talking back with choice words. Near the middle of the 12-round bout, Trotman got upset at Luftspring for what he perceived to be an unfair call and threw a right hand at the ref in anger.

That was a mistake. Luftspring may have been in his late 50s, but he never forgot his boxing training. He countered Trotman's right with a vicious left and then a heavy right that knocked Trotman out cold. Gray was given the victory by disqualification while Trotman's trainers tried to bring him back from dreamland.

Chuvalo Versus Clay at the Gardens

When the fight between Cassius Clay (later known as Muhammad Ali) and George Chuvalo was first announced, scheduled to take place at Maple Leaf Gardens on March 29, 1966, most boxing writers almost unanimously denounced it as a farce. Chuvalo was not considered a top fighter anywhere near Clay's stature, and to make matters worse, Chuvalo had lost three of his last four major fights against much lesser opponents. The only impressive credential to many of those writers was that Chuvalo had never been knocked down in the 11 career fights he had lost.

But let's not forget that the social climate for Clay wasn't all that kind either. His image in the United States was suffering after he had associated himself with the Nation of Islam and made the famous wisecrack about his draft status during the Vietnam War: "I ain't got no quarrel with them Viet Cong." While American fight fans were willing to forgive Clay's eccentricities in the past, his avoidance of the draft totally soured the mystique that had previously surrounded the champ. He could not find a venue that had a welcoming crowd, so he had to travel out of the country for a fight. However, despite all the negative press regarding his moral character, no one ever questioned Clay's fighting ability. Before the fight even started, the sportswriters were already crowning Cassius Clay the victor.

Some 4000 fans packed into Maple Leaf Gardens to scream their support for Chuvalo as he plodded out to his corner, followed by the grand entrance of Clay. The fight did not start out well for Chuvalo, taking six punishing jabs before managing to land one wild left hook to Clay's midsection that forced the champ to take a step back. It went on like this for the entire fight: Clay kept dancing and jabbing, and Chuvalo kept taking all the hits but kept attacking stubbornly, refusing to back off. It seemed inevitable that Chuvalo would fall if he continued to take such punishment from Clay's fists. Yet Chuvalo remained on his feet for the full 15 rounds.

Although his face was bloodied and grotesquely swollen, Chuvalo continued to fight back until the final bell rang. The judges unanimously gave the fight to Clay, but it was Chuvalo who walked out the true victor. Nobody had ever suspected for a minute that Chuvalo would be able to hold his own in the ring against Clay, but his performance against overwhelming odds earned him the respect of the sportswriters who had written him off before. At the post-fight press conference, a bruised Chuvalo stared out at the throng of reporters through the bluish slits that had once been eyes and took the first question.

"Were you ever in trouble?" one reporter asked.

"He never hurt me," said George. "I'd like another crack at him. I feel I've earned it." Chuvalo managed to smile through the questions and invited all the reporters to the Prince George Hotel for drinks.

When Clay emerged from the dressing room, the image could not have been more different. Flanked by three Muslim friends in their trademark bowties and suits, Clay looked like he had not even been in a fight, with not a single visible scratch on his body. Yet instead of his usual fiery oratory about how great he was, Clay had nothing but respect for the man he had just fought. "I warned you," he said. "But, you wouldn't listen. Chuvalo is the toughest man I've ever fought. Tougher'n Liston, Patterson, Jones and all the rest. His head is the hardest thing I've ever hit." Clay then showed his only injury—a pair of very swollen hands.

Shawn O'Sullivan

At the 1984 Olympics in Los Angeles, Toronto-native Shawn O'Sullivan clearly beat American boxing opponent Frank Tate in the gold medal final of the light middleweight class. Tate was twice given a standing eight count by the referee during the fight, but he somehow managed to come out ahead on points over O'Sullivan in the end. The crowd booed the judges mercilessly, but the decision stood, and O'Sullivan had to settle for the silver medal.

A Successful Toronto Sports Franchise? No Way!

At least one Toronto professional sports franchise can provide the championship-deprived city something to cheer about. The Toronto Rock of the National Lacrosse League (NLL) was founded in 1998 and, since then, has won six championships. This high level of success is unheard of in a city that has not seen a Stanley Cup in over 40 years and counting, has not won a World Series title since 1993 and whose basketball team simply struggles to maintain a .500 winning percentage.

The Toronto Rock franchise was originally known as the Ontario Raiders and was based out of Hamilton. Playing their first game at Copps Coliseum, the Raiders closed out their inaugural season with a respectable six wins and six losses, just missing out on the playoffs. However, the team was never really a big draw in Hamilton, so at the end of the season, the club was sold to a group of investors and relocated to Toronto, where they were renamed.

The move seemed to do the team a world of good as they won their division and defeated the Rochester Knighthawks 13–10 in the championship game in 1999. The club went on to win the championship in 2000, 2001, 2002, 2003 and 2005. In 2004, the team had a pretty good excuse for breaking their streak as head coach Les Bartley was diagnosed with cancer and had to excuse himself from his coaching duties. When the Rock won the championship in 2005, Bartley succumbed to his cancer the next day. In his honour, the NLL named the Coach of the Year Award the Les Bartley Award.

Eventually, the Rock came back down to Earth after so many years of domination, and in 2006, they balanced out their season with eight wins and eight losses. They squeaked into the playoffs only to get booted out early by the Knighthawks. Things got worse in 2007 when the club posted their first losing season on record, winning only six games and losing 10. The 2008 season was no better when they again finished the season below .500 and didn't make the playoffs. In 2009, the rebuilding process began. Coaches were fired, new ones were hired, players were traded and some were let go. All the changes paid off, and just two seasons later, in 2011, the Rock went all the way to the NLL championship again and beat the Washington Stealth 8–7 to claim another title, tying the Philadelphia Wings for the most NLL championships.

Go George Go!

No one expected the 17-year-old son of a Toronto cleaning woman to be a threat, but George Young went on to defeat 102 of the world's best swimmers in the 1927 Wrigley Marathon Swim. After almost 16 hours in the water, 5000 spectators greeted the young swimmer, chanting his name and crowding around just to get a glimpse of his tired frame. For his troubles, his prize was $25,000.

Young's accomplishment was truly worth the money he earned. Swimming the 35-kilometre-wide channel between Santa Catalina Island and the coast of California is considered by many swimmers to be even more difficult than swimming the English Channel. The waters tend to be very cold despite its location in the warm area of the Pacific Ocean, and the channel is constantly being swept by powerful tides and currents. Prior to George Young's feat, no single person on record had ever swam its length. Before the 1927 race, it had taken a 15-man team, swimming in relays, more than 23 hours to complete the arduous journey. Yet Young did it in 15 hours and 46 minutes.

In the first stage of the marathon swim, Young took an early lead, using his long powerful stroke to outdistance his closest competitors by several kilometres after only a few hours of swimming. Part of the reason for Young's incredible speed was probably his overwhelming fear of the abundant shark populations in the waters. He had been told prior to the race that the sharks were not known for attacking humans, but he found little comfort in that when a large great white shark followed him for several hours at the beginning of the race.

After several hours in the choppy waters, many of the swimmers dropped out of the race. Charles Toth and Henry Sullivan had both previously swum the English Channel, but they were forced out of the California waters because of exhaustion. The fact that a 17-year-old kid was still in the race electrified the crowd, and Young emerged from the waters an instant hero.

It would be great if Young's story ended there, but his fame had a high price. He was soon in high demand across Hollywood, making appearances at movie premieres and even entertaining film contracts worth $250,000. However, he was still too young to handle his affairs, so his mother signed an agreement with Henry O'Byrne giving him 40 percent of everything George earned in return for managing his career. Seeing dollar signs written all over the popular swimmer, O'Byrne was unscrupulous in his negotiations, even turning down the $250,000 movie offer because he thought the figure was too low. Even Young's $25,000 prize money was locked up into a trust fund for him, tucked away until he turned 29. Then the rumours began to circulate that Young did not actually swim the entire race himself. People could hardly believe a 17-year-old unknown had beaten the world's best marathon swimmers.

After a few months of trying to capitalize on his celebrity, Young got frustrated with his dreams of stardom and returned to Canada, where he faded into the history books. For that one herculean effort as a 17-year-old, Young was inducted into the Canadian Sports Hall of Fame in 1955.

Tackling the English Channel

How does a 16-year-old girl from Toronto prepare for her goal of swimming across the English Channel and back? By first swimming across Lake Ontario, of course. That's what Cynthia Nicholas did in 15 hours and 10 minutes in 1973.

Four years later at the age of 20, she was finally ready to attempt her goal. On September 7, 1977, she slipped into the frigid waters of the English Channel, battled through choppy waters and mental and physical exhaustion until she reached the shores of France, only to turn back around and swim all the way back.

It took Nicholas 19 hours and 55 minutes to complete the circuit, becoming the first woman to accomplish this amazing feat of strength and will. She later swam across the Channel on 19 different occasions, earning her the nickname "Queen of the Channel." For her incredible efforts, she was named to the Order of Canada in 1979 and, in 1993, was inducted into the Canadian Sports Hall of Fame.

The Cyclemaniac: Steve Bauer

Raised in Fenwick, Steve Bauer's hometown later became part of his cycling nickname, "The Fenwick Flash." Starting out as a member of the St. Catharines Cycling Club, Bauer officially began his amateur career on the Canadian national cycling team in 1977, competing in the team pursuit. He remained on the team for several years before finally deciding to strike out on his own, turning pro in 1984 after winning a silver medal at the Olympics in Los Angeles in the men's road race event.

Bauer continued his successes on the pro circuit, placing third at the World Professional Road Race in Barcelona in 1985. This event was only one in Bauer's long list of accomplishments, which included a Canadian-best fourth-place finish in the 1988 Tour de France. In that race, he won the first stage of the event and got to wear the highly coveted yellow jersey for five days. Bauer was only the second Canadian in the history of the prestigious Tour de France to ever wear the jersey; the first was Alex Stieda in 1986. Bauer repeated that feat at the 1990 Tour de France, this time wearing the jersey for nine days.

But Bauer's career was not without its difficulties. At the 1988 World Championship Road Race, he collided with Belgian cyclist Claude Criquielion close to the finish line as they raced in for the gold medal. Bauer ended up being disqualified, and then Criquielion sued him for $1.5 million in damages. After five long years battling in court, Bauer was finally acquitted of all charges. He faced another heartbreak at the 1995 Tour de France when Bauer's teammate Fabio Casartelli died in a crash with other riders during the Tour. Casartelli's head struck a set of concrete blocks alongside the road, and he died en route to the hospital.

By 1996, racing had begun to takes its toll on the veteran rider, and after placing a disappointing 41st in the Atlanta Olympics road race event, Bauer could read the writing on the wall. In October 1996, he retired as Canada's highest ranked professional road racer and the only Canadian to lead the Tour de France on two separate occasions. Although retired, he still remains active in the cycling world and opened up a business called Steve Bauer Bike Tours, which offers clients biking tours of the Niagara region as well as international destinations.

The Incredible Conacher

Born in Toronto in 1900, Lionel Pretoria "Big Train" Conacher was Canada's greatest athlete of the first half century. Raised in a household with enough money for just the essentials of life, Conacher realized early on that sports could be his ticket out of poverty.

At 6-foot-1 and weighing 200 pounds, Conacher was a natural athlete in build and also had the determination of mind to work hard for what he wanted. He earned the nickname "Big Train" because with a little hard work, he could do it all. Hockey, football, baseball, wrestling, lacrosse, boxing, you name it—Conacher was an all-round athlete who excelled at every sport he tried, an athlete the likes of which Canada has not seen since his passing. He wasn't just some dumb athlete either—he displayed skill, grace, dexterity, intelligence, determination and fair play in every sport he played.

His list of accomplishments is vast. At 16, he was the Ontario wrestling champion in the 125-pound class. At 20, he won the Canadian lightweight boxing championship, the first time he stepped into a competitive arena. Conacher even fought Jack Dempsey when the boxing great passed through Toronto in 1921. Conacher didn't win, but he gave the champion Dempsey a tough time in the ring.

In 1922, Conacher hit the run-scoring triple in the final inning of the Ontario Baseball Championships that gave the Toronto Hillcrest team the victory. After celebrating the win, he sped across town to play in the Ontario Lacrosse championships on the same day. Arriving a little late, his team was already behind 3–0. Conacher joined in and went on to score four goals and assisted on another to give the Toronto Maitlands a 5–3 win.

As if that wasn't enough, Conacher also was a member of the Toronto Argonauts in 1921 when they defeated the Edmonton Eskimos to win the Grey Cup. However, of all the sports Conacher set his sights on breaking into, the hockey world was first and foremost. In those days, hockey was the one sport that actually paid its athletes well enough to live, and he knew that if he wanted to make a career out of sports, he would have to make it into the NHL.

Only taking up skating at the age of 16, Conacher was not the best of skaters, so instead, he focused his attention on how the game was played. As a defenceman, Conacher figured out all the angles for covering his goal and could stop any fast-moving forward from breaking around him. He used his big body to block countless shots. His tactics worked, finally getting the attention of the NHL. From 1925 to 1937, he played for the Pittsburgh Pirates, the New York Americans, the Chicago Blackhawks and the Montréal Maroons. But again, Conacher didn't stop there—he went on to win two Stanley Cups, one in 1934 with the Blackhawks and the other in 1935 with the Maroons. Lionel even urged his brother Charlie to follow in his footsteps. Charlie joined the Toronto Maple Leafs in 1929 and formed the famous "Kid Line" with Joe Primeau and Harvey Jackson.

Lionel Conacher retired from professional sports in 1937. He had achieved a level of greatness in sports that no one has ever come close to matching, but he paid a heavy physical price for all those years as an athlete. He received an estimated 600 stitches from hockey injuries alone, with 150 on his face and head, and he broke his nose eight times.

Although he quit sports and found a quiet job as a Member of Parliament, Conacher never gave up playing sports, literally, until the day he died. On May 26, 1954, he drove from Toronto to Ottawa to play in the annual softball game between Members of Parliament and the press gallery. There was nothing Conacher enjoyed more than beating up on the reporters. In the sixth inning, he smashed the ball into left field, scoring one runner, and he huffed his way in for a triple. A few seconds later, Lionel Conacher toppled to the ground and died from a massive heart attack. He was 54 years old.

Notes on Sources

Book Sources

Batten, Jack. *The Leafs: An Anecdotal History of the Toronto Maple Leafs*. Toronto: Key Porter Books, 1994.

Berger, Howard. *Maple Leaf Moments*. Toronto: Warwick Publishing, 1994.

Coleman, Charles L. *The Trail of the Stanley Cup*. Sherbrooke: Progressive Publications, 1969.

Cox, Damien and Gord Stellick. '67: *The Maple Leafs, Their Sensational Victory, and the End of an Empire*. Toronto: Wiley, 2004.

Diamond, Dan, ed. *Total NHL*. Toronto: Dan Diamond and Associates, 2003.

Donald, Dewey and Nicholas Acocella. *Total Ballclubs: The Ultimate Book of Baseball Teams*. Toronto: Sport Media Publishing, 2005.

Drake, Stephen. *Weird Facts about Canadian Football*. Montreal: Overtime Books, 2009.

Edit. *Macleans. Canada Our Century in Sport*. Markham: Fitzhenry & Whiteside, 2002.

Finnigan, Joan. *Old Scores, New Goals: The Story of the Ottawa Senators*. Kingston: Quarry Press, 1992.

Judd, Ron C. *The Winter Olympics*. Seattle: The Mountaineers Books, 2008

Leonetti, Mike. *Maple Leaf Legends*. Vancouver: Raincoast Books, 2002.

McFarlane, Brian. *Best of the Original Six*. Bolton: Fenn Publishing, 2004.

Neyer, Rob. *Rob Neyer's Big Book of Baseball Blunders*. New York: Simon & Schuster, 2006.

Wallechinsky, David and Jaime Loucky. *The Complete Book of the Winter Olympics*. Toronto: Sports Media Publishing, 2005.

Wong, John Chi-Kit. *Lords of The Rinks*. Toronto: University of Toronto Press, 2005.

Web Sources

www.boston.com/zope_homepage/sports/marathon_archive/history/1901_globe.htm
www.cfl.ca
www.curtharnett.ca/Curt_Harnett_bio.htm
www.databaseolympics.com
www.mlb.com
www.nll.com
www.skatecanada.ca
www.stevebauer.com/bauerpower/aboutsteve/steve_bauer_bio.pdf

J. Alexander Poulton

J. Alexander Poulton is a writer, photographer and genuine sports enthusiast. He's even willing to admit he has "called in sick" during the broadcasts of major sports events so that he can get in as much viewing as possible.

He has earned his BA in English literature and his graduate diploma in journalism, and has over 35 sports books to his credit, including books on hockey, soccer, golf and the Olympics.